LEGAL
BRIEFS

The Ups and Downs
of Life in the Law

Edited by Roger M. Witten

PROSPECTA PRESS

Hardcover ISBN 978-1-63226-137-3
eBook ISBN 978-1-63226-138-0

Published by Prospecta Press
An imprint of Easton Studio Press
PO Box 3131
Westport, CT 06880
(203) 571-0781
www.prospectapress.com

Book and cover design by Barbara Aronica
Cover and interior image from Shutterstock AI

This book is dedicated to the many
family members, teachers, friends, and colleagues
who have enriched my life immeasurably.

CONTENTS

SECTION III—EXPERIENCES

INTRODUCTION

Who knew lawyers had good stories to tell about the ups and downs of their lives in the law, and that those stories would make enjoyable reading for the general public, as well as for legal professionals? This book is just that—a curated anthology of twenty-four short essays written by distinguished lawyers that, in plain English, tells stories that are interesting, moving, and/or amusing. Its title is "Legal Briefs" because the essays are law-related and short.

Let me assure you—you do not need to be a lawyer to enjoy these stories. Some are tongue-in-cheek. Others are serious but never dull. Some discuss historical public events. Others do not. You will find proverbial pearls of wisdom in many of them. Their variety defies any attempt to find an arc or theme that connects one with all the others. So, while one reader may wish to read this volume from beginning to end, another reader might prefer to graze. But by all means it is worth reading them all.

The subject matters of these stories are diverse and compelling. Taken individually or together, they reflect the ups-and-downs of a life in the law. The book is divided into three sections, but many of the essays would fit in two or all three sections.

Section One is called "Events." The section begins with an

essay I wrote about efforts to enact and defend the constitutionality of much-needed campaign-finance reform. The second
essay, written by Dan Marcus who was the General Counsel of
the 9/11 Commission, provides an insider's view of the give-and-
take between the White House and the Commission. The third
and fourth essays are first-hand accounts of the negotiations that
led to the release of the American hostages in Iran by two participants in that drama, Robert Mundheim and Richard Davis. Next
comes Henry Hecht's personal recollections of his involvement
in prosecutions conducted by the Watergate Special Prosecution
Force. Stuart Gerson, a Department of Justice veteran, addresses
the heavy responsibilities of prosecutors when a public figure is
a subject of investigation—a topic that will clearly resonate in
light of recent events. Finally, Trevor Potter returns to the topic
of campaign finance in a blistering critique of the Federal Election Commission, which he once chaired.

The subject matter of Section Two is "People." It begins with
an essay of mine about Watergate Special Prosecutor Archibald
Cox (on whose staff I served) and the "Saturday Night Massacre."
The next article, by Andrew Tannenbaum, is a highly personal
account of the effect the tragedies of 9/11 and its aftermath had on
federal appeals court Judge Wilfred Feinberg. Next in line is Jim
Quarles's reminiscences about the legendary Boston trial lawyer
James St. Clair in the context of a somewhat wacky case. Then
we have Dick Janis's chronicles of the defense of indicted Iran-
Contra figure Albert Hakim. Next are Carol Lee's reminiscences
and insights about former Supreme Court Justice John Paul Stevens, for whom she clerked. Lou Cohen tells of the good works of

two legal giants—Lloyd Cutler and Charles Horsky. In the next essay, Bill Kolasky treats us to a bit of history, as he recounts the tangled tale of Senator John Sherman, the nation's first trust-buster. Nelson Johnson tells a seamy story about dirty politics in New Jersey (who knew) in which patrician lawyer Arthur Van-derbilt and "Boss" Frank Hague are the principal characters. The section ends with my essay about a very unusual client.

The third Section is called "Experiences." Harriet New-man Cohen opens the section with the riveting story of a highly unusual child-custody case she successfully tried. Mar-tha Minow's contribution explores a situation where the client's interest in defeating a lawsuit was in tension with the lawyer's desire to establish a new precedent. Michael Helfer reports on two delightful and unusual court appearances. Warren Cooke's entertaining essay recounts his adventures doing a large transac-tion in Zaire. Following on the theme of international law prac-tice, I contributed an essay about my own adventures abroad. Next come two pieces, one by Mark Kessel, and another by Marty Kaplan about their first cases. The final section and the book close with one more essay by me.

The top-tier lawyers who wrote this volume's "Legal Briefs" mostly are friends and colleagues from college, law school, the Watergate Special Prosecution Force, my law firm, now known as WilmerHale, the board of the Campaign Legal Center, our thirty years in Washington, D.C. and our twenty years in New York. They are all highly capable lawyers with sterling reputa-tions—and they have good stories to tell. Each chapter begins with a short biography of that chapter's author.

SECTION I

EVENTS

1

For One Brief Shining Moment

by Roger M. Witten

BACKGROUND

In reaction to the campaign finance abuses revealed in the
Watergate scandal, Congress in 1974 amended the Federal Election Campaign Act (FECA) to strengthen its provisions regulating campaign contributions to and expenditures by individuals.
(Earlier laws had banned such contributions and expenditures
by corporations and labor unions.)

In early 1975, opponents of campaign finance reform sued,
challenging the constitutionality of the FECA, arguing that its
restrictions on campaign donations and expenditures infringed
on the First Amendment's guarantee of Freedom of Speech.

During my time as an Assistant Watergate Special Prosecutor, I learned a lot about campaign finance laws. It so happened
that just at the time I joined Wilmer Cutler & Pickering, the
League of Women Voters retained the firm to defend the FECA's
constitutionality in court. Given my prior experience, I joined
the team as a junior lawyer.

The Supreme Court in 1976 delivered a mixed opinion in

the case, which was called *Buckley v. Valeo*. The Court held that the First Amendment was not violated by reasonable regulations of contributions to candidates, but that expenditures by citizens to support a candidate that were not coordinated with the candidate's campaign were protected speech.

In the years following the Supreme Court's decision, both parties and their candidates exploited loopholes in what remained of the FECA, rendering it ineffective. One such abuse, referred to as "soft money," involved federal officials and candidates raising money from corporations and large donors ostensibly for use in unregulated state elections. In fact, soft money was used, at least in part, to support or oppose federal candidates. Another abuse, known as "sham issue ads," involved broadcast advertisements that purported to be constitutionally protected speech about an issue, but were actually thinly disguised electioneering messages that supported or attacked candidates.

MCCAIN-FEINGOLD BIPARTISAN CAMPAIGN REFORM ACT

In response to these abuses, Senator John McCain—one of the few Republicans who championed campaign-finance reform—worked across the aisle with Senator Russ Feingold, a Democrat, to draft the Bipartisan Campaign Reform Act, known informally as "McCain-Feingold" (or BCRA). After several efforts to enact the bill failed, Congress in 2002 passed the bill and President George W. Bush signed it. Curiously, President Bush signed this landmark legislation without holding a signing ceremony and without inviting Senators McCain and Feingold to the White House.

It had been clear for some time that, if Congress enacted

McCain-Feingold, the law would be challenged in court. Accordingly, the law's sponsors and a coalition of supporters began preparing for the court battle before Congress passed the law.

One delicate question they confronted was: who would lead the court defense. Over the years I had deepened my campaign finance law expertise. I worked on campaign contribution investigations as a member of the Watergate Special Prosecution Force and litigated, pro bono, numerous campaign-finance cases while in private practice. A number of people aspired to the position, but several members of the reform group thought I should lead it.

They arranged for me to meet with Senator McCain. We met on the Hill. Mindful that he was a busy guy and didn't like orations, I confined myself to just one sentence: "Senator, if you can get this bill passed, we will defend it and we will win." He didn't ask any questions. I must have said the right thing, as soon thereafter I was selected to lead the team representing McCain, Feingold, and their co-sponsors.

The law, as enacted, included two unusual procedural provisions. First, the bill provided that members of Congress had a right to participate in the litigation as a party. This was important because it effectively required that the court that would hear the case would permit us to participate as a full-party defendant, and not merely in the more limited capacity of an *amicus curiae*. This was crucial because it was unclear whether the Bush administration would allow the Department of Justice to defend the law, and there was concern that any DOJ defense of the law might not be as passionate or robust as the defense we intended to mount.

Second, the law provided that the case would be heard

initially by a three-judge district court with a direct appeal to the Supreme Court (in contrast to the usual procedure, which is for cases to be heard first by a single district-court judge, then by a three-judge appeals court, and then by the Supreme Court if it chose to hear the appeal).

MCCONNELL V. UNITED STATES

As expected, a slew of parties—including Senator Mitch McConnell, the NRA, and the ACLU—sued the day President Bush signed the bill into law. The various lawyers on the plaintiff's side jockeyed for position, each wanting the decision, which they expected would invalidate the law, to bear their client's name. The lead plaintiff ended up being Senator McConnell, and the case has been known as *McConnell v. The United States* ever since.

The press called the plaintiffs' lawyers "the dream team," because it included such luminaries as Ken Starr, Floyd Abrams, Charles Cooper, Jan Baran, and Bobby Burchfield. This stirred our competitive juices, since our team was not exactly made up of hacks. To the contrary, it included, among others, Seth Waxman (former Solicitor General), Randy Moss (now a federal judge), Burt Neuborne (renowned NYU law professor), "Fritz" Schwartz (legendary Cravath partner, Brennan Center leader, and full-time sage), Fred Wertheimer (of Common Cause and Democracy 21 fame), Trevor Potter (former FEC Chairman, counsel to Senator McCain, and later founder of the Campaign Legal Center), and Josh Rosenkranz (Brennan Center lawyer), not to mention the brilliant and incredibly devoted team of junior lawyers at WilmerHale and other firms and organizations.

The members of our coalition were committed to the

successful defense of the BCRA, but were not always on the same page as how best to conduct the litigation. While my focus remained on the merits, I spent a fair amount of energy acting like an air traffic controller, trying to keep the sixty-two supersonic legal eagles on our team from crashing into each other. The DOJ and the Federal Election Commission did mount a defense of the BCRA, which was welcome, but created further coordination challenges.

All the lawyers on our team agreed on one strategic point: the key to the defense was to build a detailed-factual record of the rampant abuse, corruption, and appearance of corruption that was so debilitating to our democracy. We needed these facts to support our legal argument stating that there was a demonstrable compelling need for each provision of the BCRA. Such a showing was necessary in providing a factual predicate for the legal conclusion that these provisions did not violate the First Amendment's protection of speech. We did not want to give the Justices any leeway to decide the case based on any pre- or mis-conceptions they may have had about the extent, severity, and impact on the functioning of our democracy of the abuses the BCRA addressed. The plaintiffs took the outlandish position that there was no need for the court to have a full set of facts before it.

At the hearing before the three-judge court on this important issue, we managed to persuade them to our way of thinking. Giving us a critical strategic victory, the court allowed the litigants to build a factual record—that was the good news. The bad news was that the court gave us a very short deadline to complete the work. We all worked frantically over the next weeks, and achieved our objectives more or less.

After this fact-gathering phase of the case had been completed, the three-judge court held a hearing on the merits in a packed ceremonial courtroom in Washington, D.C. The "dream team" ably made its arguments. Seth Waxman, Randy Moss, and I argued for the BCRA sponsors. The court upheld portions of the law, but struck down other provisions. We immediately appealed to the Supreme Court, as did the other parties.

As we approached the Supreme Court argument date, Seth Waxman graciously inquired whether I wanted to split the oral argument with him. In response, I asked Seth how many Supreme Court arguments he had previously made. The answer, as I recall, was thirty-three. I thanked Seth for his thoughtfulness and said that since his Supreme Court experience was exactly thirty-three cases greater than mine, and since this case was so important, it would be the wrong time and place for my first Supreme Court test drive.

The oral arguments in a packed Supreme Court were vigorously presented on both sides. Seth made a strong argument. The Justice's questions did not provide a basis for confidently predicting the result.

But when in 2003 the result was announced, it was cause for jubilation. The Court upheld the constitutionality of every single provision of the statute. Validating our strategy, the Court's opinion emphasized "the reams of disquieting evidence in the record [which] convincingly demonstrates. . ." and the "unmistakable lesson from the record in this litigation." Justice Sandra Day O'Connor cast the deciding vote to uphold the BCRA. The "dream team" had lost. Senator McConnell had given his name to a losing case.

DOWNHILL FROM THERE

That was the highpoint. Some years later, the composition of the Supreme Court changed. In the infamous *Citizens United* case, the Court, over our objections as an *amicus curiae*, effectively overruled *McConnell*. Since then, it has been very challenging to persuade courts to uphold measures to curtail the rampant abuses that pollute federal and state elections. With an apparently entrenched conservative majority on the Court, it may take a generation before the folly of *Citizens United* can be rectified.

2

The White House and the 9/11 Commission

by Daniel Marcus

Daniel Marcus graduated from Brandeis University and Yale Law School. He clerked for Judge Harold Leventhal on the U.S. Court of Appeals for the District of Columbia Circuit. His career in private practice was spent entirely at Wilmer Cutler & Pickering in Washington, D. C. Dan also had several stints of public service. During the Carter administration, he was Deputy General Counsel of HEW and General Counsel of the Department of Agriculture. In the Clinton administration, he was Senior Counsel in the White House Counsel's office and then Associate Attorney General of the U.S. Later, he became General Counsel of the 9/11 Commission.

THE 9/11 COMMISSION

In the wake of the 9/11 attacks—the most traumatic event for Americans since Pearl Harbor—there were calls, particularly from the families of the victims, to create an independent commission to investigate and report on what happened, what caused the attacks, and what steps could be taken to prevent such events in the future. The Bush administration and many Republicans in Congress resisted the idea, but after a long fight led by

Senators Joe Lieberman and John McCain, Congress approved the creation of an independent bipartisan commission in the fall of 2002. Fatefully, as we shall see, the statute provided that the Commission would be located in the legislative branch rather than the executive branch of our government.

The Commission was chaired by Tom Kean, the former Governor of New Jersey. Former Congressman Lee Hamilton was Vice Chair, and the remaining commissioners were equally divided between Republicans and Democrats. I served as General Counsel.

In short order, I was plunged into difficult and time-consuming negotiations with lawyers in the White House Counsel's office. Our requests included: 1) interviews with high-level White House officials and cabinet officers and their testimony at public hearings, and 2) access to top-secret National Security Council (NSC) documents and CIA briefings to the president (the now famous Presidential Daily Briefs or PDBs). At the outset we were met with resistance based on the related doctrines of Separation of Powers and Executive Privilege.

The Separation of Powers doctrine grows out of the Constitution's allocation of various powers to the three branches of our government—the executive, legislative, and judicial branches. Under the doctrine of Executive Privilege, which the Supreme Court has recognized, the president and other senior officials of the executive branch may in certain circumstances decline to produce information where production of the information would cause harm and/or chill candid advice.

Alberto Gonzales, then Counsel to the President, worried that if the White House granted access to information in its possession to the Commission, a legislative-branch agency, it would create a precedent that would hamper the White House in its future dealings with Congress. His concerns were shared, to some extent, by the Office of Legal Counsel (OLC) in the Department of Justice.

We argued that the happenstance of the Commission's "location" in the legislative branch was irrelevant: the Commission was a one-time only investigative entity that had no legislative powers that should trigger a Separation of Powers analysis. For months, this argument met a stone wall. Therefore, a number of compromises had to be negotiated, along with the adoption of euphemisms insisted on by the White House.

First, we made a few tactical concessions: We did not initially press to interview the President or Vice President, and we agreed not to seek documents that were direct communications to either President Clinton or President Bush. Also, we did not ask witnesses questions about conversations with the President.

We got lucky. It turned out that the key NSC memoranda on counterterrorism and the Al Qaeda threat were from Richard Clarke, the NSC's counterterrorism chief, to the National Security Advisor (Sandy Berger in the Clinton administration, Condoleezza Rice in the Bush administration). Berger regularly replaced Clarke's name as the author of the memos with his own, and sent them on to President Clinton. Thus the Clarke memos we had access to effectively told us what advice the president received. And Rice did not typically communicate to President Bush in writing.

We reached a compromise with the White House lawyers on access to NSC and other top secret White House documents. The

White House lawyers refused to allow such sensitive documents, which never would be given to a congressional committee, to leave the grounds of the Executive Office of the President. So we agreed to examine NSC and other White House documents in a Sensitive Compartmented Information Facility (SCIF) they established for us in the New Executive Office Building around the corner from the White House (and convenient to our downtown location in unlabeled office space provided to us by the CIA). Even though we all had top-secret security clearances, only commissioners, senior commission staff members such as me, and a couple of designated staff members, could visit the SCIF and review the highly classified documents.

Under a painstakingly negotiated treaty with the White House Counsel's office, we were allowed to take notes on the documents in the SCIF, but could not take the notes back to our office (even in a classified carrying case, and even though our office was also a SCIF). Moreover, the notes we took could not "substantially recreate" a document. This led to some amusing disputes: Our best staff researcher on the NSC documents, a PhD historian, was an avid notetaker. The White House lawyer who reviewed his notes insisted that many of them violated the "Substantial Re-creation Rule" and that we therefore could not use them. I convinced him (barely) on several occasions to make allowances for the zeal of an academic researcher and vowed to curb his notetaking excesses in the future.

My biggest coup concerning our notes of NSC documents occurred in the waning days of the Commission, when we were rushing against a statutory deadline to complete our report. We needed to bring the notes from the White House SCIF to our office, in violation of the treaty, to write our report. "Oh no," said the White House lawyers. "You can go to our SCIF and write that portion of the report consulting your notes there." I finally convinced them to indulge the fiction that we would be merely "borrowing" our notes, which would remain the property of the executive branch and would be promptly returned after we drafted our report.

Euphemisms and face-saving restrictions also came in handy to assuage White House concerns about our interviews with high-level White House officials and cabinet members. We agreed that the interviews would be called "meetings"; they would not be recorded or under oath, and they would be conducted only by a commissioner, the Commission's executive director, or me.

This last restriction assured me of one of the most interesting experiences of my professional career. Since Executive Director Philip Zelikow had worked on the Bush transition team for the NSC and co-authored a book with Condoleezza Rice, the chair and vice chair decided that, while Zelikow would conduct the "meetings" with senior Clinton administration officials, I would conduct the "meetings" with sitting Bush Administration officials—Rice (the National Security Advisor), Stephen Hadley (her Deputy), White House Chief of Staff Andy Card, Secretary of State Colin Powell, Secretary of Defense Donald Rumsfeld, Secretary of the Treasury John Snow, Attorney General John Ashcroft, and Secretary of Homeland Security Tom Ridge.

The White House initially took a hard line about White House officials testifying in public at commission hearings. Under long-standing practice—endorsed by the Justice Department—

officials such as the National Security Advisor are not made available to testify before Congress on policy matters. Therefore, they said, Rice could not appear as a public witness. (At least one commissioner wanted us to subpoena her, but we held off on the "nuclear option.")

Once again, we got lucky. At a nationally televised Commission hearing on counterterrorism policy in the Clinton and Bush administrations, our star witness was Richard Clarke, the former NSC counterterrorism deputy, who had just published a book on counterterrorism policy in the Clinton and Bush administrations—and appeared on CBS's *60 Minutes* touting it. His dramatic testimony before the Commission was highly critical of the Bush administration and his NSC bosses for failing to take the Al Qaeda threat seriously enough before 9/11. In the aftermath of the hearing, and unbeknownst to us at the time, NSC Director Rice insisted to the White House counsel and the President that she be allowed to testify publicly to rebut Clarke's testimony.

Out of the blue, a letter from White House Counsel Gonzales to Chair Kean and Vice Chair Hamilton arrived. The letter executed a complete about-face in the White House's position. Not only did it say that Rice would be allowed to testify in a public commission hearing, but it granted another longstanding request: The commission would be permitted to interview President Bush and Vice President Cheney jointly at the White House.

Gonzales's letter went on to take the legal position opposite to the one that the White House lawyers had previously taken: that allowing Rice to testify publicly and the commissioners to meet privately with the President did *not* constitute a precedent for the White House's future dealings with Congress because the Commission was not a legislative body. Remarkably, Gonzales's letter went on to ask that the Commission affirm that its access to Rice and the President did not constitute a precedent for the White House's dealings with Congress.

At the public hearing, Commissioner Richard Ben-Veniste, a former Watergate prosecutor, asked Rice a cleverly phrased question that elicited the disclosure of the explosive title of a PDB delivered by the CIA to President Bush a month before the 9/11 attacks—"Bin Laden Determined to Strike in the United States." (We knew the title already, but Ben-Veniste could not state it himself because the PDB was classified top-secret.) Shortly after Rice's testimony, the White House declassified and released that PDB (the now famous August 6 PDB) so that the world could see that it was not quite as scary as its provocative title suggested.

This emboldened us to press our document request to the CIA for all PDBs relevant to the Al Qaeda threat, which in turn led to a final saga of White House resistance and eventual agreement to another treaty with the Commission that we successfully exploited. The White House told us that there were some 300 PDB items responsive to our request, but only about twenty that they deemed important to our investigation. But they refused to grant us access to any of them, on the ground that the PDBs were top-secret communications of critical intelligence information to the President (and a few other senior officials) and never shared with any member of Congress.

Instead, they offered us a CIA briefing for the commissioners and senior staff on the twenty "important" PDBs. The CIA briefing was a disaster; every commissioner agreed that it was totally unsatisfactory.

So we embarked on a lengthy but ultimately successful negotiation of another "treaty" with the White House Counsel's office. Under the treaty, the core group of twenty PDBs would be examined by a "review group" consisting of the Commission chair and vice chair, plus one additional Democratic and Republican commissioner or senior staff member. Two members of the review group (the commission designated Commissioner Jamie Gorelick and Executive Director Philip Zelikow) would then be allowed to view all 300+ PDBs responsive to our request to see whether any of them should be added to the core group of twenty PDBs, after which the review group would then prepare a "concise summary" report on the enlarged-core group that would be made available to all commissioners and the senior staff. Both the switch of additional PDBs from the larger pool to the core group and the summary report to the full Commission and senior staff required approval by the White House counsel— an approval under the treaty "not to be unreasonably withheld."

The White House lawyers, advised by OLC, viewed this negotiation and treaty to be in the tradition of "accommodation" employed by the executive branch in seeking to avoid the need for the president to invoke executive privilege as the basis for refusing to turn over documents to congressional committees.

Of course, Gorelick and Zelikow pushed the envelope on adding PDBs to the core group, and they wrote a "concise" summary that sorely strained the idea of conciseness. Twice—first, when it looked like we would be unable to reach agreement on the treaty, and second, when the White House lawyers threatened to reduce sharply the number of PDBs to be added to the core group, and to refuse to approve the "concise summary" report prepared by Gorelick and Zelikow, the Commission considered issuing a subpoena for the PDBs or for the extensive notes taken by Gorelick and Zelikow.

Fortunately, the White House lawyers caved on both points. I say "fortunately" because I am convinced that the White House would have refused to comply with a subpoena, leaving us only with the alternative of filing an enforcement action in federal court that could not conceivably have been resolved before the Commission went out of existence a few months later.

Our success in gaining significant access to the PDBs and obtaining the public testimony of National Security Advisor Rice made some important "law on the ground." The exaggerated mystique of the PDBs was punctured; the widely read 9/11 Commission Report demonstrated that we could have public disclosure and discussion of intelligence information provided to the president in the past without jeopardizing the ability of the intelligence agencies to operate effectively. Similarly, Rice's public testimony established an important precedent that may be reflected in future OLC opinions and court decisions. As policymaking in the executive branch continues to move from cabinet departments to the White House, it becomes less plausible to regard officials such as the National Security Advisor exclusively, as confidential advisors to the president rather than policymakers in their own right, who should be accountable to Congress as well as independent commissions.

The 9/11 Commission Report, which was cleared by the White House and the intelligence agencies, even though it contained a great deal of information that had been highly classified until that point, was a great success. The report sold more than a million copies and was a finalist for the National Book Award. And Congress and the executive branch implemented almost all of our recommendations, including a massive reform of the intelligence agencies.

3

Who Knows What Will Happen Next?

by Robert Mundheim

Robert Mundheim graduated from Harvard College and Harvard Law School and has received an honorary masters from the University of Pennsylvania and honorary doctorate degrees from the New School and the University of Arizona. Bob is a man of many accomplishments. Among them: Special Counsel to the SEC, General Counsel of the U.S. Treasury, co-Chair of the Fried Frank law firm, of counsel at Shearman & Sterling, University Professor of Law & Finance at and Dean of the University of Pennsylvania Law School, General Counsel of Salomon Inc., and member of ten business and six non-profit boards.

GETTING TO TREASURY

I was a professor at the University of Pennsylvania Law School, teaching corporate law and securities regulation, when in 1976 I took a leave to teach for a year at UCLA Law School. I wanted to teach corporate governance there, but thought it would strengthen the offering if I could persuade a professor at the UCLA Business School to teach it with me. I called the Dean of the Business School, Harold Williams, and told him about my idea. He said that it was a good idea and that he would teach it with me in the spring term.

In late December, Dean Williams called me to say that newly elected President Carter had asked him to become the Chairman of the Securities and Exchange Commission (SEC). He told President Carter he would take the position. Therefore, he could not teach the Corporate Governance Course with me. However, he pointed out that there would be a vacancy in the commission, and he would recommend that President Carter appoint me to fill it. I was delighted at the thought of such a prestigious appointment in a role in which I thought I had some expertise.

Two months later, Dean Williams called to say that he had recommended my appointment as an SEC Commissioner to the White House. Their response was that I was eminently qualified and that if my name was Roberta, they would gladly appoint me. I was deeply disappointed with the news.

Before I got too depressed, I received a call from Bob Carswell whom I got to know during a brief stint at Shearman & Sterling and when we both worked in Washington in the Kennedy administration (he at Treasury, I at the SEC). Carswell had been nominated as the General Counsel of the Treasury, but had been made Deputy Secretary when the prior nominee for that position had stepped aside. Carswell asked me if I would be interested in becoming General Counsel of the Treasury. Although I realized that there were many areas at the Treasury in which I had little or no knowledge, I told him I was interested. The White House was willing to make this appointment.

AT THE TREASURY

Serving as the General Counsel of the Treasury Department was very broad and I had much to learn.

As a young associate, at the SEC, and as a professor, I had never managed anyone other than myself. I now had 1,100 lawyers at the Treasury ultimately reporting to me.

The new position required a different approach than I used before. For example, almost every day I would receive memos for transmittal to other senior Treasury officials or others that I was asked to sign. As an academic, I read and carefully edited any memo or article to which my name was attached. Using that approach at the Treasury, my inbox grew higher and higher even though I arrived at work earlier and left later. I soon realized that my approach to signing memos would have to radically change. And it did. If the conclusion seemed correct and appropriately worded, I signed the memo and moved on to the next one.

I had many difficult and interesting problems to resolve as Treasury General Counsel. Among them were the Chrysler bailout, the freezing of Iranian governmental assets when American hostages were seized, the negotiation of the claims and assets agreement as a necessary final step before the formal US recognition of China. A few months after arriving at Treasury, I was asked to add to my responsibilities leading the group in charge of anti-dumping and countervailing duties. Japanese televisions, Polish golf carts, and Mexican tomato exports were the most challenging matters.

THE HOSTAGE NEGOTIATIONS

One of the most important assignments occurred in January 1981. I had left the Treasury on September 1, 1980 and returned to the law school at the University of Pennsylvania to teach. At the beginning of the second week in January, Bob Carswell called to tell me that he thought there was a chance that a deal could be negotiated to free the American hostages held in Iran. There had previously been a number of promising efforts, but all had gone nowhere.

Although I was scheduled to start teaching classes soon, I agreed to try to help. The proposed deal was that we would get our hostages, and the Iranians would get a return of their frozen assets. Since neither side trusted the other, the first question was how to set up the trade. When would we turn over the assets we had frozen? The Iranians would want their assets in neutral hands (an escrow agent) who would transfer the assets as soon as the hostages left Iran in a neutral aircraft.

The first choice as escrow agent was the Bank of England and my first assignment was to talk to them. The bank staff with whom I met were unenthusiastic about the bank acting as escrow agent, and gave many reasons why the bank could not do it.

My next stop was to try the Deutsche Bundesbank. Its staff thought the bank could play the needed role.

I flew back to London where a meeting with Prime Minister Thatcher had been set up by the US Ambassador. When we met the next day, Prime Minister Thatcher said she wanted to do anything needed to free the hostages. At my meeting later that day with the Bank of England staff, all of the difficulties raised at the earlier meeting no longer presented a problem.

The next step was to go to Algiers to negotiate with the Iranians. The "Treasury team" included two private bank lawyers, the General Counsel of the New York Federal Reserve, the Deputy Governor of the Bank of England, and one other Bank of England official. When we entered the room where the negotiations would be held, we realized there were no Iranians in the room. They wanted no direct contact with "the agents of the Devil." The process would be that we talk to the Algerians in English and they would translate into French and then to Farsi. The Iranians would respond to the Algerians in Farsi which would be translated into French and then English. This process created a lot of room for errors and misunderstandings in the negotiations. A number of critical failures in communications occurred, and almost derailed the negotiations.

We also had a last-minute legal issue which could have blocked the consummation of the deal. The General Counsel of the New York Federal Reserve Bank believed that the bank did not have the power to carry out an important part of the transaction. This difficulty was communicated to the White House and Lloyd Cutler, the White House counsel, began to talk to the New York Federal Reserve Bank general counsel in hopes of persuading him that he could authorize the transaction to go forward.

In the midst of this discussion, President Carter intervened and said that nothing (certainly not some legal point) should prevent the closing of the deal. When the New York Fed lawyer realized who had joined the discussion, he fainted (since we had been up for forty-eight hours, the impact of this last-minute pressure was not surprising). Fortunately, the president of the New York Federal Reserve Bank had been an Undersecretary of the Treasury in the Carter administration and President Carter was able to persuade him to sign the agreement without his General Counsel's blessing.

In the end, negotiations successfully concluded in the last moments of the Carter administration. One of the thrilling moments of my life occurred when I watched the hostages disembark from the airplane which had flown them to the Algiers airport.

4

Dealing with the Iranian Hostage Crisis

by Richard Davis

Richard Davis graduated from the University of Rochester and Columbia Law School. He then clerked for Judge Jack Weinstein in New York. Davis has served in several government positions, including Assistant U.S. Attorney for the Southern District of New York, the Watergate Special Prosecution Force, and as Assistant Secretary of the Treasury. In private practice, he was a partner at Weil, Gotshal & Manges in New York. Rich has received numerous awards and has served on a host of organizations promoting good government

When I arrived at the Treasury Department in August 1977 to assume my position as Assistant Secretary (Enforcement & Operations), I understood that I would face many difficult challenges. After all, I supervised the Customs Service, the Secret Service, the Bureau of Alcohol Tobacco & Firearms (BATF), the implementation of the Bank Secrecy Act and the Federal Law Enforcement Training Center, while also dealing with broader law enforcement policy issues. And I was going to be supervising far more senior agency heads despite the fact that I was only thirty-one years old. Having law enforcement experience and being perceived as non-political was of significant help. However, I was not wrong about the challenges I would face.

During the first twenty-seven months of my tenure, I engaged in a brutal, and losing, fight with the National Rifle Association (NRA) over some proposed, very modest firearms regulations, and dealt with some thorny and controversial issues relating to BATF's regulation of the alcoholic beverage industry. I endured the stress of monitoring how the Secret Service protected the president and others, and most recently dealt with the high risks involved in the Secret Service's protection of Ted Kennedy, as he became the third and the last surviving Kennedy brother to run for president, and numerous death threats aimed at Fidel Castro when he visited the United Nations. Customs also presented numerous issues, ranging from controversial customs penalty cases, developing money laundering investigative strategies, the perpetual problem of policing thousands of border miles, prevention of drug smuggling, and airport processing issues. With all these challenges and more, my days, nights, and weekends were more than full.

Then, on November 4, 1979, my life changed. The U.S. Embassy in Iran was seized, and a 444-day hostage ordeal began. As the crisis developed, economic sanctions became the principal way the government sought to put pressure on Iran to release the hostages. One of my other responsibilities was to oversee the Office of Foreign Asset Control (OFAC), an approximately fourteen-person office whose core responsibility was to implement those sanctions. Its primary weapon was to freeze the assets of foreign governments and their citizens, which means that all transactions in any assets in which the object of the freeze has an interest—bank accounts, accounts receivable, and any other type of property—would be prohibited without a license from OFAC. Prior to November 4th, I had spent very little time on OFAC issues. That soon dramatically changed.

In recent times there has been an effort by some to disparage the work of long-time government employees by referring to them as "deep state." For me, however, these employees represent the historical memory and experience which is essential to the successful functioning of the government, particularly in times of crisis.

And that certainly was the case in November of 1979. Within a day of the hostages being taken, and when it was still hoped this would be a short-term crisis, Stanley Sommerfeld the long-time Director of OFAC, came to see me. Stanley understood that at times of international crisis, presidents often turn to non-military alternatives to demonstrate strength, and to retaliate in response to hostile actions. And economic sanctions were the principal weapons in this toolbox. Stanley thus suggested that we begin drafting the necessary executive orders and implementing regulations so we would be ready if the call came from the White House. I agreed.

In the first few days, we worked without policy guidance, and thus the early drafts were extraordinarily broad, covering the Iranian government, government-controlled entities, and Iranian nationals. After a few days, however, we discussed the various policy issues with the senior Treasury officials and then with the White House, the New York Federal Reserve, the State Department, and the Justice Department. As a result, when the call came very early in the morning of November 14th, we were ready. I came to the office before 7 a.m., the Executive Order was signed by President Carter at 8:10 a.m., and the implementing regulations were issued shortly thereafter.

It is difficult to describe what my life was like over the next fourteen months. Some days, virtually all of my time was devoted to dealing with the hostage crisis, and on an overall basis more than two-thirds of my time involved working on Iranian issues. For approximately six months, my day began with an early morning meeting that included Deputy Secretary Bob Carswell, the Treasury General Counsel Bob Mundheim, one of his Assistants, and the Treasury liaison to the intelligence community. After six months, these meetings took place three times a week. At these meetings we would receive an intelligence briefing and discuss the policy issues associated with implementation of the sanctions, and later on questions relating to how the sanctions might be unwound in a resolution of the crisis. These meetings would also prepare Bob Carswell for his follow-on meetings at the White House. During these fourteen months, I participated in many hundreds of meetings, some with representatives of other departments and the National Security staff, some with others at the Treasury, and others with representatives of banks, oil companies, and others impacted by either the sanctions or by Iranian actions.

But before I could effectively perform my responsibilities, I had a lot to learn. I was selected for my position largely because of my law enforcement experience, and it is fair to say that my knowledge of the banking system and financial transactions was limited. To help educate me as we navigated the many issues arising under the sanctions, particularly in the early days, Ernie Patrikis, Deputy General Counsel of the New York Fed, became my tutor, spending countless hours in my office in the first months after the freeze was imposed. Among other things, he helped me think through the impact on the banking and international financial system of various policy choices. And, of course, I regularly worked with Bob Mundheim and Bob Carswell, an experienced banking lawyer, who became the Treasury's lead person on Iranian hostage issues.

There had been other sanctions programs involving the freezing of assets of foreign governments and nationals. But in two fundamental ways, the Iranian freeze was very different, and far more difficult to administer. First, earlier freezes involved at most, several hundred million dollars of assets. The Iranian freeze captured over ten billion dollars of assets. Moreover, even though the Shah had been overthrown some ten months earlier, there was still a very large number of ongoing transactions and banking relationships which were impacted by the freeze. More significant was the reality that we had to constantly evaluate the impact of what we were doing, on the hostages. Would a particular action add to the pressure on the Iranians to end the crisis, or would it increase the risks to the security and lives of the hostages? The fact that lives were at stake was always present in our minds as we decided how to implement the freeze, and this increased the pressure we felt every day.

There is not enough space in this essay to describe the countless issues which needed to be addressed in administering the sanctions. I will instead discuss a few examples to provide a sense of the issues we faced.

One issue that needed to be confronted in drafting the initial regulations was the extent that the freeze would cover individuals and overseas subsidiaries of U.S. entities. In the days before the freeze was implemented, in discussions within Treasury it was decided to include only assets of the Iranian Government and government-owned entities. Given the fact that the state-owned companies (the oil company, for example) and banks controlled the vast majority of overseas assets, excluding individuals and private entities, would not materially diminish the effectiveness of the sanctions. In addition, the experience with the Cuban regulations, where assets of individuals had been frozen, taught OFAC about the complexities of dealing with a steady stream of refugees whose assets had been frozen. Also, there was an understanding that the Iranians were demanding a "return" of the Shah's assets, and while we did not know what assets he and his family had in the U.S., we did not want to create the impression, by freezing individual assets, that the U.S. government could, in fact, seize, rather than freeze any of their assets and turn them over to Iran.

Another challenge we had to address both in drafting the initial and later regulations, was how to maximize the pressure on Iran while maintaining the strong support of our allies. The principal issue in striking this balance was the extent to which the freeze would apply to overseas branches and subsidiaries of U.S. companies. Doing so would plainly antagonize our allies since other countries traditionally resented the U.S. government trying to control the activities of entities licensed by and operating within their borders. In the initial regulations, we decided not to include subsidiaries, but when it came to the branches of

U.S. banks, particularly those in London and Paris, we believed the amounts involved were simply too great to exclude from the freeze. And we turned out to be right. Based on consultation with the New York Fed, we believed that billions of dollars were at stake, and in the end the number turned out to be approximately 5.6 billion dollars. Iran sued in London and Paris, challenging the application of the freeze to these deposits. We were concerned how courts in these countries would ultimately rule. By pushing for delays and enlisting the UK and French governments to help secure delays, no court issued a ruling by the time the crisis ended fourteen months later.

The issue arose again in April 1980 when the U.S. imposed a formal export embargo on transfers to Iran. While the freeze largely interrupted trade with Iran, the U.S. had attempted to secure a UN Security Council resolution imposing an international trade embargo. But after its invasion of Afghanistan, the Russians vetoed the resolution. The President thus decided we should announce our own export ban and encourage other countries to do the same. Here it was understood that the U.S. imposing its ban on foreign subsidiaries of U.S. companies would be met with strong objections from our allies. It was thus decided not to do so, at least not directly. Instead, companies were required to provide notice to OFAC prior to their subsidiaries exporting to Iran.

Our strategy was simple. Once we received a notice, or more often a call or meeting to discuss sending such a notice, I would tell the company that while such exports were not prohibited, the Treasury's position was that the required notice could be publicly released under the Freedom of Information Act. Given the high emotion within the country generated by the holding of the hostages, U.S. companies did not want it to be known that their subsidiaries were still trading with Iran, so almost no such exports went forward.

Not further jeopardizing the safety of the hostages was always a core consideration in any decision. It was partly the reason why, after a U.S. lawyer for the Iranians met with Bob Carswell and me immediately after the freeze was imposed, the decision was made to license Iranian embassy and consular accounts.

Protecting the hostages was a central part of how we addressed the issue of payments to the many thousands of Iranian students studying in the United States. These students were largely dependent on stipends they received from relatives in Iran, and while their accounts were not frozen, the accounts of the Iranian state-owned banks through which the stipends were processed were subject to the freeze. One image which we did not want to see was television footage of Iranian students talking about their inability to pay their rent or buy food. As a result, a license was issued to the U.S. branch of an Iranian bank allowing new money to be transferred through the bank to Iranian students. We thus avoided providing an excuse for Iran to mistreat the hostages because we were mistreating Iranian students. At the same time because of the risks involved in allowing these payments—we didn't really know the backgrounds of the students, and many had been involved in anti-Shah protests before his ouster—records of each payment were required to be sent to OFAC, which forwarded them to the Justice Department.

Over the ensuing months we dealt with a large number of issues. How to address the litigations filed by Iran in London and Paris, the extent to which we would allow U.S. claimants to resort to U.S. courts to sue Iran (we allowed them to secure pre-judgment attachments but actively sought to prevent judicial decisions about their validity), how to deal with standby letters of credit issued by U.S. banks, and many more.

At the same time, we met with banks and oil companies, both to make sure that they understood their obligations under the sanctions, and to obtain a better understanding of the amount of frozen assets that they controlled.

As time passed, and back-channel diplomacy failed, a few things became clear. First, any ultimate agreement to release the hostages would be complicated. Simply undoing the freeze, which had been in place for many months, would no longer mean that Iran would gain immediate access to its blocked funds. Pre-judgment attachments in the U.S. and the right of banks to hold onto funds in light of Iran's default on loans were among the reasons that made this impossible.

In late April 1980 came one of the worst moments of the crisis. I was in Glynco, Georgia presiding over a meeting of the Federal Law Enforcement Training Center, which I chaired, when shortly before dawn I was called to take a call from the Treasury, where I was told a military effort to rescue the hostages had ended in total failure. Not only was the news depressing, but it meant that the path forward to securing the release of the hostages was very uncertain.

The period from late April until September of 1980 was focused on continued sanctions issues, meeting with numerous interested parties, and trying to get a more accurate picture of the precise amount of assets caught up in the freeze, and the dollar value of claims against Iran. Among other things, a formal census was undertaken which required all U.S. persons and entities to report the amount of frozen assets they were holding and the amount of any claims they had against Iran. To get comfortable with the accuracy of the reporting we conducted meetings with the major holders of assets and claims. But one thing we did do is always understate the amount of frozen assets whenever we spoke publicly (e.g., by saying in excess of seven billion dollars). We were anticipating a negotiation and did not want to be in a position where the Iranians demanded the return of more assets than actually were frozen.

The negotiating process which ultimately led to the release of the hostages included moments of optimism and moments of despair. There had been an attempt at a resolution before the rescue mission, with some French lawyers and the president of Panama serving as intermediaries, but that attempt failed. Then in September, the Ayatollah announced four prerequisites for the release of the hostages: a pledge by the U.S. not to intervene in Iran's internal affairs, return of the frozen assets, cancellation of U.S. claims against Iran, and return of the Shah's wealth.

While, other than the first condition, these demands could not literally be met, later proposals by the U.S. purported to address each one of them. At the same time, a core position that we needed to maintain in any negotiations was that the government would not pay ransom. In this context it meant that any agreement could not put U.S. claimants in a demonstrably worse position than they would otherwise be in.

The next pass at a resolution took place in September, when through the assistance of the German government, a meeting was held there between a U.S. delegation led by Deputy Secretary of State Warren Christopher, and including Bob Carswell, with a relative of the Ayatollah. While with the onset of the Iraq-Iran war that channel disappeared, it was clear that the Iranians were looking to end the crisis. After all, they had successfully used the hostage crisis to displace the Shah with a government ultimately controlled by the more radical religious clerics. And, after the Iraq invasion they both wanted access to the frozen assets and some support from the international community as a victim of an invasion. Both goals were impossible as long as they held the hostages.

In the period leading up to the release of the hostages, in addition to the U.S. and Iran, there were two other key players. One was the government of Algeria and the other was the so-called "bank channel." While there had been some hope of serious negotiations taking place prior to the 1980 election, the Iranian parliament only published its version of the Ayatollah's four points a few days prior to the election. In doing so, they proposed that Algeria serve as the intermediary in any negotiations. The State Department had a positive view of the relevant Algerian officials, and the Algerians played a critical role in the months ahead. In the spring, Citibank's German lawyers had been approached by Iran's German lawyers regarding opening discussions about resolving bank claims against Iran. John Hoffman, who had been Bob Carswell's law partner, advised him of this development. The government gave John approval to proceed provided that he kept the U.S. government informed, and it was made clear to the Iranian side that no agreement could be implemented absent the release of the hostages. This bank channel proved extremely helpful, particularly in the last days of the crisis.

As the Algerians continued their shuttle diplomacy there were two key issues on which the U.S. and Iran were far apart. First, the number of the frozen assets that could, as a practical matter, actually be returned to Iran when the hostages were released. Second, was addressing the claims of U.S. persons and entities against Iran. A serious bump in the road emerged shortly before Christmas when, in violation of the understanding with the Algerians, the Iranians released the prior negotiating history and made exorbitant and impossible to meet demands that the U.S. deposit twenty-four billion dollars in escrow, with fourteen billion to ensure the return of all frozen assets, and ten billion to ensure the return of the Shah's assets. I was in a meeting at the State Department when these demands were received and the reaction was a combination of shock and depression. But Deputy Secretary of State Warren Christopher saw two critical positives in the Iranians' demands: the introduction of the concept of an escrow account and their suggestion of some form of international arbitration agreement to deal with claims. Christopher and the President thus decided to proceed to try and reach an agreement prior to January 20, 1981.

In January, events moved quickly. We recognized that if there was to be an escrow account, we needed an escrow agent. In early January, Bob Mundheim, who had left the Treasury to return to Penn Law School, was recruited to go to Europe to find one. After talking to the central banks of Germany and the UK, he ended up negotiating with the Bank of England. And as January 20 approached, he moved to Algiers where he joined Warren

Christopher. As the Algerian shuttle diplomacy seemed to be making progress, Christopher had gone to Algiers on January 7 in an attempt to speed up the negotiations. Bob Mundheim was at some point joined by Ernie Patrikis representing the New York Fed.

From the time Bob left for Europe and Christopher went to Algiers, my life became non-stop Iran hostage crisis. Between receiving status reports from Bob first thing New York time (EST), and with events happening in London, Algiers, Tehran, New York, and Washington virtually twenty-four hours a day, I was getting about four hours of sleep a night. In the last seventy-five hours before the end of the crisis, I survived on a one-hour nap on my office couch.

In the meantime, between Bob Carswell and me, we were in constant contact with the banks trying to firm up the precise amounts they held, monitoring negotiations in New York between the banks and Iran's lawyers over the interest rate the banks would pay on the frozen deposits, and talking to other claimants. We worked with the State Department as they drafted an international arbitration protocol, met with others in the government about a variety of issues, including how to address the domestic bank deposits covered by pre-judgment attachments, and constantly revised necessary documentation to reflect what we were hearing from Algiers.

At the same time, with the Reagan administration poised to take over, we were briefing the incoming Deputy Treasury Secretary on progress. It was clear that they were both eager for us to reach a deal and wanted to maintain sufficient distance so they could not be held accountable for any concessions that were being made.

One of the major issues that needed to be addressed was how to make available the Iranian deposits at the overseas branches of the U.S. banks. Just ordering the banks to waive their rights and release them while they were owed many billions of dollars could, in effect, be viewed as ransom. For months, negotiations through the bank channel had failed, and these negotiations became part of the official negotiations in January.

On January 15, things seemed to come together. Iran dropped its demand to $8.1 billion to be returned on release of the hostages, and in a reversal from its earlier position, told the Algerians that they would repay $3.5 billion of "problem free" loans and create an escrow to deal with $1.5 billion in "problem" loans. We immediately contacted the banks, told them of this proposal and said we needed a very senior bank executive from each bank with decision-making authority to come to Washington the next morning.

The meeting was at the State Department with the Secretaries of State and Treasury in attendance. We had determined the night before that Iran's categories roughly matched the amount of syndicated loans which were very unlikely to involve problems—about $3.6 billion—and loans by individual banks—about $1.4 billion. At the meeting, I watched as the banks agreed to this categorization and very senior executives took out calculators and provided us with the precise dollar amounts they were holding, and the amount of interest each bank owed, to satisfy the Iranian demands.

From January 16 on, there was a mad dash, and by the afternoon of the 19th we thought there was a deal: $7.955 billion would go into escrow—$5.6 billion in overseas bank deposits,

$2.35 billion in Iranian assets held by the New York Fed, and a small amount of Iranian money held by the Defense Department. Once the hostages were released, about $3.6 billion would go back to the New York Fed to pay off all the syndicated loans, about $1.4 billion would go into an escrow account, while any issues as to those loans were resolved by negotiation or a newly created International Arbitration Panel. That Panel was principally created to deal with claims by U.S. entities, and by Executive Order those claims could no longer be able to be pursued elsewhere. It would be funded with an initial $1 billion from the domestic bank deposits once those were freed from the pre-judgment attachments, with an obligation of Iran to add to that amount over time. The U.S. pledged not to interfere in internal Iranian affairs, and as to the Shah's assets if Iran sued to recover assets in the U.S., we would freeze those assets pending the outcome of the litigation, and agree that the Shah and his family no longer benefited from sovereign immunity.

Relief, however, soon turned to dismay as a dispute arose over a technical document designed to implement the arrangements with the banks and the terms of an attached payment instruction which Iran would give the banks. As Iran threatened to scuttle the deal, efforts to resolve the issue proceeded on two fronts—through the official channel with Bob Mundheim in the lead, and through the bank channel. At a certain point that night I was in Bob Carswell's office minding the store while he went home for a shower. I received information that it looked like the bank channel would produce a resolution with a new payment instruction while eliminating the technical document. Bob called in to discuss the status of his discussions regarding the technical document. The issue was whether he should proceed or we should just rely on the bank channel solution. I took a deep breath and told Bob to abandon his negotiations. My extreme nervousness over whether I had made the right decision was relieved when moments later Bob Carswell and Lloyd Cutler, Counsel to the President, walked into the office and concurred.

At around 2 a.m. on the 20th we were all gathered around the telex machine at the Treasury waiting for the Iranian payment instructions to arrive. When it finally did and we looked at it we saw that a transmission error had caused many of the words to be garbled. Treasury Secretary Miller read it and after a brief discussion he decided it was sufficient and authorized me to release to the bank lawyers, including those standing with us, the OFAC order directing the banks to transfer the deposits to the New York Fed who would then transfer the required $7.995 billion to the Bank of England escrow account.

Again, when we thought we were done, another issue arose. Ernie Patrikis, the New York Fed representative in Algiers, was concerned that without the abandoned technical document he could not sign the Bank of England escrow agreement. After a tense call from President Carter to him, with us listening in, with the help of the New York Fed's president and my telling Ernie since he was signing as the Treasury's agent, we were telling him to sign, he did.

We were finally done. We waited in Bob Carswell's office for the hostages to be released. As we sat at one end of the hall, exhausted and emotionally drained, at the other end of the hall there was a party of incoming Reagan officials. They waited for the inauguration and the subsequent parade, which would pass by the Treasury's window on the way to the White House. It soon became clear that Iran wanted to impose a final humiliation on President Carter by waiting until after Ronald Reagan had been inaugurated, to release the hostages. And so, shortly after noon on the 20th the plane carrying the hostages left Iran. After 444 days I could finally exhale, and several hours later headed home where I could finally sleep.

5

Richard Nixon and Me

by Henry L. Hecht

Henry Hecht attended Williams College and the Harvard Law School. He served on the Watergate Special Prosecution Force (WSPF), which is where we met. Henry has spent the bulk of his career teaching negotiations, depositions, and trial practice at the University of California, Berkeley, School of Law and designing and presenting training sessions on these subjects for law firms around the country.

EPISODE ONE

When I graduated from Harvard Law School, I was for a period unemployed, having decided that I did not want to work at a traditional law firm. My unemployment ended when I was hired by the Office of Economic Opportunity (OEO) to work in the Office of Training within the Legal Services Corporation. I thought I had found a perfect job given my interests.

Then President Richard Nixon intervened in my life for the first, but not the only time. He was determined to dismantle the OEO by defunding its programs. Although a federal judge later ruled that Nixon's effort was "unauthorized by law, illegal, and in excess of statutory authority," this ruling came too late to save my job. The Office of Training had already been defunded.

EPISODE TWO

Little did I know that a better job would soon come along, and it too would involve President Nixon. I read in the news that Harvard Law Professor Archibald Cox had been tapped to serve as the Watergate Special Prosecutor and was building a staff. I wrote to him seeking a position. My letter was in retrospect rather naive. It started "With this letter of brief introduction, I would like to express my deep interest in joining your efforts as Special Prosecutor in whatever manner I can."

A number of Professor Cox's faculty colleagues were helping him by screening job applicants. On Friday, June 15, 1973, they told me that I would be hired unless Professor Cox, after interviewing me, disapproved. During my interview with Professor Cox, he asked me about my grades during the recently completed spring semester. I had to say that I did not know because the Law School had not yet sent me my grades. Notwithstanding this, Cox offered me a position on the Watergate Special Prosecution Force (WSPF).

I started work on Monday, June 18, 1973, a date I will never forget because it also happened to be my mother's birthday. When I joined the WSPF, I was the most junior member of the legal team and the only one hired right out of law school. I had not yet taken a bar examination or been sworn in as an attorney. Every other lawyer in the office was already a member of the bar. I passed the Maryland State Bar Examination in the summer of 1973 and was sworn into the bar that fall. Professor

Cox's secretary kindly brought a cake to celebrate my admission to the bar.

Now that I was a licensed member of the bar, I was allowed to appear before the Watergate Grand Jury along with my colleagues. My incubation period was over—I was a fully authorized, albeit green, prosecutor in a very significant criminal investigation.

I served in that capacity until late 1975, by which time many of my colleagues had moved on. As best as I can tell, my tenure on the WSPF lasted longer than any other attorney on the WSPF. In any event, the stage was set for my second encounter with President Nixon.

Some explanation is needed to understand the role I played in the "Saturday Night Massacre." That background can be found in my colleague Roger Witten's essay "Prelude to a Massacre," and will not be repeated here.

On Friday night, October 19, 1973—the night before the "Massacre," I was working late and was the only lawyer still in the office. The practice was that when there were no lawyers in the office, the federal Marshals who guarded our office answered calls that came through the switchboard and made notes of the calls on a small Memorandum of Call form. As I was leaving the office, the Marshals, realizing that I was the sole prosecutor left in the office that night, gave me a memorandum of a call received earlier that evening.

The call was from Charles Alan Wright, who was a special legal consultant to President Nixon (the Memorandum of Call mistakenly stated that the caller was "Marshal Wright"). The right Mr. Wright's message was a request that Professor Cox call

Alexander Haig, the White House Chief of Staff, before 10 p.m. The Marshals advised me that Professor Cox was at his brother's house and gave me his brother's phone number. When I reached Professor Cox, he told me he had already spoken with General Haig. It may well have been the call in which Professor Cox informed the White House that he could not and would not accept the so-called "Stennis Compromise" in which the Nixon administration proposed that the hard-of-hearing Stennis would listen to the contested Oval Office tapes and report on their contents. Cox insisted on production of the White House tapes that the Grand Jury had subpoenaed.

That set the stage for President Nixon's order directing Attorney General Elliot Richardson to fire Cox and abolish the WSPF. Richardson resigned rather than fire Cox. Then Deputy Attorney General William D. Ruckelshaus refused to fire Cox and resigned. Finally, the third in the chain of command at the Justice Department, Solicitor General Robert Bork, fired Cox. Thus, as in Episode One above, it appeared that once again the President was taking action that would cost me my job.

As it turned out, while Cox was fired, the WSPF remained in operation. When this became clear over the weekend, the entire legal staff returned to the office to be greeted by one telegram, attached to a tiny pumpkin, with many more telegrams covering their desk from citizens around the country voicing support for the WSPF. Western Union reported that its Washington, D.C. office received more than 50,000 telegrams, most of them demanding the impeachment of President Nixon.

Shortly thereafter, Leon Jaworski was named as Cox's replacement. Aware of the skepticism some felt about his appointment, he met with all of us in a room referred to as the "bull pen." He introduced himself and then said "I've heard nothing but good things about you all, so let's get back to work." And we did.

The tapes were produced to the WSPF after the Supreme Court upheld the subpoena. Several prosecutors, including me, were assigned the task of listening to the tapes. Unfortunately, the tapes were of such poor quality that it was virtually impossible to decipher what was being said or who was speaking. This difficult task was therefore outsourced to the FBI.

EPISODE THREE

Sometime after the "Saturday Night Massacre," President Nixon resigned and took up residence in what had formerly been called the "Western White House" in San Clemente, California. The WSPF and grand jury were, in mid-1975, still investigating a number of issues, including whether a tax deduction had properly been taken when the former president donated his Vice-Presidential papers to the National Archives.

On June 24, 1975, the former President was questioned under oath in San Clemente because his lawyers said he could not travel to D.C. to appear before the Grand Jury because of illness (phlebitis as I recall). A compromise was worked out between the WSPF and the former President's personal counsel, pursuant to which two members of the full twenty-three-member Grand Jury would attend the interrogation of the former President in person in San Clemente as "representatives" of the Grand Jury. At that session, one of the grand jurors in attendance asked President Nixon to take the oath on his family's Bible, which he had brought with him, and the ex-President did so.

I had kept secret the testimony the ex-President gave for some thirty-six years, because that testimony was secret under Federal Rule of Criminal Procedure 6(e). In July 2011, the testimony was released to the public pursuant to a court order by a federal judge in Washington, D.C. after a Freedom of Information Act request was filed by a historian.

Several members of the WSPF posed questions on different topics to the ex-President. When it became my turn, I was introduced to him by name. He asked me if my name was H-E-C-H-T, spelling it out. I said "yes." Then he asked me if I was related to the Hecht Company, which at the time owned a prominent department store in D.C. When I replied in the negative, he went on to say that Pat and he had bought a dining room set at the Hecht Department store when he was first elected to Congress. It seemed to me that the ex-President was still using his political skills to try to make a personal connection with me, the Assistant Special Prosecutor who was examining him.

In this third episode involving President Nixon and me, he did not take any action that would leave me jobless.

EPISODE FOUR

I worked on the investigation concerning President Nixon's donation of his Vice-Presidential papers to the National Archives. He had taken a tax deduction in the amount of $576,000 pursuant to a federal statute that permitted this. One small problem, however: the statute allowing this deduction had expired before he made the donation. To solve this problem, Nixon's team backdated the Deed of Gift and the Appraisal of the papers to fit the timing requirements of the statute.

This investigation led the WSPF to bring three indictments: Edward L. Morgan, Deputy White House Counsel, who signed the backdated Deed of Gift; Frank DeMarco, Jr., Nixon's personal attorney, who co-signed the backdated Deed of Gift; and Ralph G. Newman, who signed the backdated Appraisal. Morgan pleaded guilty. Newman was convicted by a jury. DeMarco, who was indicted for making false statements to the IRS and obstructing a Congressional inquiry, pleaded not guilty and went to trial.

The presiding judge, Warren J. Ferguson, dismissed all the charges the WSPF brought against DeMarco. The judge did not find that the charges against DeMarco were insufficient to allege an offense or that the evidence would not support a conviction. Rather, unhappily, the judge found that the WSPF had not fulfilled its legal obligation to turn over to the defense before trial all exculpatory information in the prosecution's possession and that the proper remedy was a dismissal of all charges (instead of, for example, ordering a new trial). We strongly disagreed with that ruling.

What happened was this: during the trial, a former IRS agent testified that during a meeting with DeMarco and his counsel, Charles McNelis, DeMarco confessed that he backdated the Deed of Gift. McNelis informed the judge that it was he, not his client, who out of the presence of DeMarco had first acknowledged DeMarco's guilt. The former IRS agent testified that DeMarco then returned to the interview and confessed his guilt.

My handwritten notes of the meeting were among the documents the judge ordered the prosecution to produce as relevant to the factual question of "who confessed." In the judge's decision, my handwritten notes are referred to as the "Hecht Notes." The judge found that certain documents the prosecutors produced, including both the handwritten and typed versions of my notes, made no explicit mention of a confession by DeMarco himself, were in that regard exculpatory, and therefore had to be turned over to the defense, and that our failure to do so warranted dismissal of all charges. Our office's appeal to the United States Court of Appeals for the Ninth Circuit was unsuccessful.

Any case in which the WSPF is found to have engaged in prosecutorial misconduct is newsworthy and, regrettably, my name found its way into a *New York Times* story on October 9, 1975, as one of the WSPF attorneys present for the interview of DeMarco with his attorney McNelis present and as the author of handwritten notes of the meeting, which did not include a confession by DeMarco. On October 10, 1975, yet another story appeared in the *New York Times*, again including my name as an attendee at the meeting with DeMarco and McNelis. The story reported that on October 9, the trial judge dismissed all charges. I had hoped one day to have my name in the *New York Times*, but not for being the author of notes that led in part to the dismissal of all charges brought against DeMarco.

While President Nixon denied responsibility for the backdating, before he left the White House, he paid the sum of $432,787.13, plus interest, that the IRS said he owed due to the deduction he took, which the IRS had disallowed because of the backdating the WSPF had alleged.

Perhaps it was not surprising that Nixon's White House put out a statement on April 3, 1974, saying: "Any errors which have been made in the preparation of the President's returns were made by those to whom he delegated the responsibility for preparing his returns and were made without his knowledge and without his approval."

And that ended my personal encounters with Mr. Nixon.

6

Fighting Public Corruption and Serving the Rule of Law: A Prosecutor's Reminiscence

By Stuart M. Gerson

Stuart M. Gerson is a former Assistant United States Attorney, Assistant Attorney General and Acting Attorney General of the United States. When not serving in government, he practiced law at Epstein Becker & Green.

Every federal prosecutor sooner or later is compelled to reflect—and to act—upon the admonition of Justice George Sutherland in the 1935 Supreme Court case of *Berger v. United States* that:

> The United States Attorney is the representative not of an ordinary party to a controversy, but of a sovereignty whose obligation to govern impartially is as compelling as its obligation to govern at all.

Adherence to this principle might require the prosecutor to bring a controversial case against a popular public figure on his own ground. Or it might require the confession of error where the government has overreached. Or it may result in doing nothing, deciding not to prosecute if the facts are insufficient to proceed. Whatever the nature of the decision at hand, it always requires federal prosecutors to satisfy the constitutional duty, derivative of that of the president under whom they serve, to take care that the law is faithfully executed, without fear or favor, and with the utmost candor before the courts in which they practice. There is no more important, or fulfilling, duty within the public practice of law.

Besides the importance of the prosecutorial undertaking itself, one has found no greater professional or personal satisfaction than being allowed to stand before a court, having been announced as the representative of the United States. There can be no better client than our country itself and the citizens its government serves.

None of this is to say that the Department of Justice and the thousands of lawyers it employs at its headquarters and in the ninety-four federal judicial districts always do the right thing. The historical examples of the Teapot Dome scandal, the Watergate era and, more recently, in its leadership having given cover to authoritarian actions of a now-defeated ex-president, demonstrate that DOJ does not always trail clouds of glory. But most of the time it does, and its line lawyers are capably and faithfully serving the public in cases of importance and complexity, often having made considerable financial sacrifices to do so.

But there are warning signs that this might be changing.

Over the last half-century, I have seen that many of the smartest, most creative and public-service-oriented recent law school graduates and judicial clerks have been drawn to DOJ's litigating divisions and to the offices of the United States Attorneys. Lately, however, one sees signs from both the political left and right that many young lawyers are rejecting the prosecutorial role.

On the left, echoing critical studies and deconstructionist curricula that have become entrenched in many law schools, a significant number of young lawyers whose predecessors might eagerly have sought prosecutorial positions to start their immediate or post-clerkship careers, not only reject, but openly condemn, the prosecutorial function as a perpetrator of the unjust enrichment of the economically-privileged and, perhaps overlooking who actually are the disproportionate victims of crime, of pursuing institutionally racist law enforcement tactics and decision-making.

From the right, echoing certain congressional partisans whose views seem to originate in conspiracy theories and selective factual analysis, some young lawyers condemn DOJ and its prosecutors, along with the Federal Bureau of Investigation, as somehow having "weaponized" law enforcement to the end that selective prosecution targets purported conservatives while giving a pass for analogous conduct on the part of progressives.

Critics of both sorts display more intensity than they do facts. Far more often than not, American federal prosecutors distinguish themselves and the nation in fighting corruption among the privileged and fighting crime that disproportionately victimizes the poor and members of minority groups. Where they haven't, their colleagues and successors have energetically corrected matters.

As I am in the twilight of a long and diverse legal career, which I intend to continue for as long as my mental faculties hold out, I'll take a little time to recount several matters that a young prosecutor experienced, and that shaped his belief that ethical prosecution is not only a linchpin of a fair and well-ordered society, it is an occupation that provides as much personal satisfaction as it does service to the public.

THE SHADOW OF WATERGATE

Every new scandal, real or imagined, seems to have the word "gate" appended to it. The grandparent of them all was "Watergate," the burglary of Democratic National Committee Headquarters located in the Watergate Hotel complex by agents of Richard Nixon's reelection campaign, and the coverup that followed that led to Nixon's resignation in the face of likely impeachment and conviction.

The scheme unraveled when, in the early morning hours of June 17, 1972, a security guard named Frank Wills spotted duct tape covering an office lock, and alerted police who were able to apprehend five men who were charged with burglary and communications eavesdropping.

Prosecution of this first wave of defendants was assigned to a team of prosecutors in the Office of the United States Attorney for the District of Columbia led by Earl Silbert, Seymour Glanzer, and Donald Campbell. Among the things that were learned early on in the grand jury investigation, and through contemporaneous *Washington Post* reporting by Bob Woodward, was that a check for $25,000 that was generated by a midwestern official of The Committee to Reelect President Nixon ("CREEP"), had been filtered through Miami, and ended up in the hands of Maurice Stans, former Secretary of Commerce and the chair of the Finance Committee to Reelect the President ("FCREEP"). That money appeared to have been used to finance the conspiracy, and its discovery laid the matter smack in the middle of the Nixon campaign. That is the sort of broth that attracts many cooks.

I was a rather junior Assistant United States Attorney when I received a call from Earl Silbert, the office's principal assistant and leader of the prosecution team. He informed me that the district attorney of Dade County, Florida, had filed a motion in the Superior Court of the District of Columbia seeking what, in essence, was the extradition of Stans to Florida under the Uniform Act To Secure the Attendance of Out of State Witnesses. Silbert asked me to represent the federal government in opposing what the prosecutors saw, not incorrectly, as a hot-dog move by a state prosecutor seeking to put himself in the limelight. Stans was an important witness in the federal prosecution, and Silbert believed that his investigation would be materially impeded if the Florida, DA were to succeed. I cobbled together some opposition papers and, following a hastily called hearing, Judge Paul McArdle agreed with our position, and Stans stayed in Washington. Thus, I became a minor footnote in Watergate history as the first person to represent the government in a litigated case in the matter.

Because my office was in the federal courthouse, I was able to attend some of the Watergate trial sessions. The original prosecutorial team led by Earl Silbert acted with distinction and effectiveness but for reasons of a political and policy nature, was displaced by Special Prosecutor Archibald Cox who, following the "Saturday Night Massacre," was succeeded by Leon Jaworski. His staff secured guilty verdicts on the charges against, among others, John Ehrlichman, former White House domestic policy advisor, and John Mitchell who had chaired Nixon's reelection campaign after holding the position of Attorney General.

Ehrlichman's trial counsel had a grating personality that had offended both judge and jury and he was found guilty. After his conviction, Ehrlichman changed his lifestyle greatly and took a new tack as his sentencing approached. He left his wife and moved to New Mexico, where he began working to assist the Indians at the Taos pueblo. He then brought in new counsel, Ira Lowe, a left-wing lawyer and activist organizer, to allocute on his behalf. His urging to Judge Sirica that Ehrlichman be sentenced to public service with Indian organizations was to no avail, as "Maximum John" lived up to his nickname.

As John Mitchell's lawyer Bill Hundley related it to me, Mitchell, whose sentencing was to come later and who had never prevaricated concerning the conduct of which he was found guilty, listened with bemusement to the Ehrlichman discussion and, observing that it had Judge Sirica's eyes rolling, turned to his lawyer and said: "Hundley, if they offer me the reservation, turn it down." That ended my brief connection with the Watergate prosecution but not, as it turned out, with people who were involved in it.

VOUCHING FOR THE CREDIBILITY OF A DISGRACED NATIONAL LEADER WHILE FIGHTING DRUG CRIME

I'd learned a good deal already about maintaining both diligence and objectivity in managing the prosecutorial function. My dealings with John Mitchell, which were not connected to Watergate, taught me more.

Title III of the Omnibus Crime Control and Safe Streets Act of 1968 was a comprehensive attempt by Congress to promote the effective control of crime, a major political issue during the Nixon administration, while protecting the privacy of individuals, especially as to their thoughts and expressions. Thus, the statute sets forth an elaborate procedure intended to satisfy constitutional mandates by which governmental officials can obtain court orders to conduct electronic surveillances upon detailed, documented factual representations in certain serious cases, but which prohibits the unauthorized interception of oral and wire communications except pursuant to such a court order.

Obtaining that order requires the prior review and approval of a constitutional officer, who may not delegate those responsibilities to a lower-ranking person. Accordingly, a Title III wiretap application must identify the Attorney General, or an Assistant Attorney General specially designated by him, and they are the only persons empowered to authorize the application.

The provenance of such wiretaps soon became an important issue in several cases before the Supreme Court of the United States. In *United States v. Chavez* in 1974 the Court ordered the suppression of evidence in a case where Attorney General Mitchell's executive assistant, a career DOJ functionary named Sol Lindenbaum, albeit after a telephone conversation with his boss, gave the actual authorization for the application at issue. And in a companion 1994 case, *United States v. Giordano,* the Court reached a similar result where the warrant at issue misidentified the Assistant Attorney General, Will Wilson, as having authorized a Title III application.

There was a third case in the mix, and it involved John

Mitchell himself, and the resolution of the wiretap warrant application found him serving as a pro-government witness at the same time as he was a criminal defendant in the Watergate case.

"Reds" Scott was a Washington, D.C. drug kingpin. Pursuant to a Title III wiretap conducted over a one-month period, government agents intercepted a large number of phone calls over a phone that was being used in furtherance of a conspiracy to import and distribute narcotics. This led to the conviction of a number of conspiracy members including its leader, Mr. Scott.

Following arraignment, the U.S. Attorney assigned the case to me and my colleague, the late Roger Adleman, a very capable career prosecutor. The district court judge in the case was Joseph Waddy, an elderly and crusty jurist. And the first thing we had to deal with was a motion to suppress evidence on the same basis that informed the *Chavez* and *Giordano* cases: that the warrant application was not authorized in fact by the putative signatory to the document. That person was Nixon's notorious Attorney General, John Mitchell.

At the outset, it appeared to Adelman and me that we weren't going to have much trouble proving that Mitchell had authorized the application. Indeed, his signature appeared on the questioned document, and he himself was available on a daily basis in the same D.C. Courthouse where his Watergate trial was proceeding before Judge John Sirica. In fact, Judge Sirica's courtroom was directly across the hall from Judge Waddy's and there were numerous breaks in the trial that allowed us to meet with Mitchell and his lawyer, the legendary D.C. trial attorney, Bill Hundley.

With the aid of a Metropolitan Police Department handwriting analyst named Jimmy Miller, we were able quickly to get handwriting exemplars from Mitchell to compare with the signature on the application. The only problem was that Miller concluded that the questioned signature did not match the specimens. That surprised everyone concerned and so we went back to Mitchell, whom Adelman and I had gotten to know during our earlier meetings, where he was quite loquacious in speaking about his tenure as Attorney General and his law practice before it. Mitchell was adamant that he in fact not only authorized the Scott warrant application but had signed it. He knew, and had been annoyed, about the disposition of the two Supreme Court cases and remembered the Scott case particularly because it arose at about the same time as the other two cases, and the name of its protagonist "Reds," not "Red" as might seem typical, stayed with him.

So, we got some new exemplars from Mitchell for comparison. Same result. Miller could not see a match. Same rejoinder. Mitchell was insistent and complained that Miller, one of the best known and best qualified handwriting examiners in the country, was "nuts."

We didn't give up. As Adelman and I investigated the matter further, we learned that Mitchell, who had been a naval officer in World War II, had suffered a war injury that created a worsening nerve impairment in his hands. Moreover, he was under a great deal of pressure during the Watergate trial, less from the case itself (as I'll explain a bit later) than from his deteriorating family situation. As he was being tried, his marriage to Martha Mitchell, who had become a notorious public figure in her own right, was fracturing, and the former AG was concerned that their young daughter might be kidnapped and sequestered by the combative Martha. Mitchell's concern was credible enough that Judge Sirica would adjourn his trial early on Fridays so that Mitchell, who was free on bond, could fly home and assure the security of his daughter.

Because Mitchell exhibited a tremor in his hands, we hypothesized that perhaps from the time he claimed to have signed the warrant application to the time we were obtaining new specimens, his signature somehow had changed. Jimmy Miller was more than skeptical of this theory, but we went both to DOJ and to Mitchell's former law firm and got documents from an earlier time that irrefutably bore his signatures. We also met with Sol Lindenbaum, who confirmed Mitchell's recollection of events and provided exemplars of his own handwriting so that he might be ruled out as having been the Attorney General's amanuensis, as he improperly had been in *Chavez*.

Mitchell's handwriting indeed had changed, and so had Jimmy Miller's opinion. Both Mitchell and Miller ultimately testified, and Judge Waddy upheld the warrant and its fruits. "Reds" and his accomplices later were tried and convicted and, after several bouts at the Court of Appeals for the D.C. Circuit, their convictions were finally affirmed by the Supreme Court.

During the events just recounted, the U.S. Attorneys Office was at the same time in one courtroom convicting Mitchell of political corruption and in another courtroom across the hall from the first, vouching for his probity. Fortunately, the rule of law was upheld in both courtrooms.

PROSECUTING A CORRUPT U.S. SENATOR—NO FAVOR TO THE WEALTHY OR WELL-PLACED

As a young prosecutor, I was charged with the prosecution of a popular sitting U.S. Senator, Daniel Brewster of Maryland. It was at that point, the most significant case to which I had been assigned.

Brewster had run up considerable debt in serving as a surrogate for Lyndon Johnson in fending off a primary challenge by Alabama's segregationist governor, George Wallace. In his effort to deal with that debt, Brewster had accepted payments from the Spiegel catalog mail order company, paid with the intention of using his position on the Senate Post Office and Civil Service Committee, to lower mailing rates. Brewster's case had made an early trip to the Supreme Court, which decided the case against him, holding that receiving bribes and gratuities was not protected by the Constitution's Speech or Debate Clause.

In the midst of my preparation, I received a call from Harold Titus, the U.S. Attorney himself, telling me that my presence had been requested by the Assistant Attorney General (AAG) for the Criminal Division, and that I was to attend a meeting about the case the next day at "Main Justice," the colloquial name for the Department's DOJ's headquarters. I was not yet steeped in the politics of DOJ. I had never even been inside the Main Justice building. So, given the importance of the case, I naturally asked "Who will be going with me?" "You'll be on your own" was the reply. And when I inquired if there was anything particular that I was supposed to convey, I was told that I'd know what to do. Really?

With some apprehension, I appeared at DOJ headquarters and was led to an anteroom in the Criminal Division where I was joined by the defendant Senator's attorney, Edward Bennet Williams, among the best known and most capable lawyers in the country, a name partner in one of the top law firms in Washington and an important political supporter of the President, a fact that gave me pause. What's more, he brought along a partner and several associates to back up his arguments that DOJ should abandon the case.

Soon an inner door opened and Henry Peterson, the Assistant Attorney General for DOJ's Criminal Division stepped out, uttered a general greeting and asked me—just me—to come to his office. He introduced himself and then simply asked whether I thought the case in question was justly brought and whether the evidence was sufficient to support a guilty verdict. I responded that we had recently "turned" a key witness and that the evidence was otherwise sound, and that we were well prepared. That was the whole conversation.

The AAG and I then walked back into the anteroom, and he turned to Williams and simply said that he had reviewed the matter with the Assistant U.S. Attorney and was satisfied that the prosecution was a just one and it would go forward. There was nothing else to say but "goodbye." The case ultimately proceeded to a successful conclusion, and I was left with an indelible understanding that the business of the DOJ was doing impartial justice, and that our cases would be brought against violators of the law, irrespective of station. And upon conviction, our sentencing recommendations would not be different for the socially or politically well-connected than they would be for others.

Henry E. Peterson, who led his division in successfully attacking organized crime and political corruption over decades, was a pillar of strength and rectitude among DOJ staff lawyers and Assistant U.S. Attorneys, but he wasn't the only one who stood as guarantor of departmental fairness. In the Criminal Division, there were senior career lawyers like Jack Keeney, David Margolis and Bea Rosenberg. In other divisions, there were career lawyers like Stuart Schiffer and Ernest Brown. There were U.S. Attorneys like Thomas Flannery in D.C. and Bob Fiske in the Southern District of New York. All of these were important influences in my career and in the careers of generations of lawyers throughout the country. Some of them became my colleagues in later years and I am forever grateful for that.

Ed Willliams and I got to know each other well during the Brewster proceedings, though he had passed the Senator off to his partner Paul Connolly, when Brewster finally pleaded guilty to a series of statutory misdemeanor counts under the federal bribery statute. Brewster entered his guilty plea before Judge George Hart, who then was the Chief Judge.

THE CONNALLY PROSECUTION

Judge Hart also was the presiding judge in a post-Watergate case brought by Special Prosecutor Jaworski alleging that former Texas governor and U.S. Treasury Secretary John Connally had accepted a bribe in exchange for his influencing the government to increase federal dairy price supports. Connally, who also was represented by Edward Bennett Williams, was charged with violating the same bribery statute under which Senator Brewster was charged and convicted.

In anticipation of the possible trial of Brewster, I had prepared an extensive trial brief and jury instructions. Although they proved unnecessary in Brewster's case, his having pleaded, Judge Hart found them useful in the Connally case.

Knowing that connection, Williams suggested that I audit the Connally trial, which I did.

Calling character witnesses, including Jacqueline Kennedy and Billy Graham, and masterfully conducting a direct examination of his client that locked every door that the prosecutors might have tried to open on cross-examination, Williams secured his client's acquittal.

I had won my battles with Williams in the Court of Appeals and District Court, but I'd concede in a second that he was the finest courtroom lawyer I ever saw. Nevertheless, while the Connally jury was deliberating, Ed Williams asked me—a much younger and less-experienced lawyer—how I thought he had done. Although he was to win the case, he was sweating the outcome then. That exercise of humility by a consummate practitioner was an object lesson that I've never forgotten.

SOMETIMES THE JUSTICE DEPARTMENT WINS BY LOSING

Much later in my career, after a long stint in private law practice, often defending cases against Justice Department staff lawyers and Assistant United States Attorneys, I was nominated by President George H. W. Bush, a friend whom I had assisted during his campaign, to return to the DOJ as an Assistant Attorney General. As President Bush's administration ended, I was asked by his successor, President Bill Clinton, to stay on as Acting

Attorney General of the United States until a suitable successor could be confirmed by the Senate. For a variety of political
and policy reasons, my new tenure continued for months before
Janet Reno became the new AG.

In describing his time as Attorney General during the Eisen-
hower administration, Herbert Brownell said that to him the job
was "just one damn thing after another." I might have enjoyed
the job more than he did, but I concede that it always seemed to
be raining controversy, whether it was the Waco siege, the first
World Trade Center bombing, questions of sexual identity in the
military, presidential war powers, or many other matters with
which I was faced.

One that proved especially controversial was the criminal
trial of Congressman Harold Ford, Sr., of Tennessee. Ford, who
represented a district that included Memphis, was an ostenta-
tious public figure who had been charged with multiple counts
of conspiracy, bank fraud, and mail fraud. He litigated his case as
much outside the courtroom as inside, waging a defense based
on charges that the government was pursuing a vendetta against
him because he was an African-American. That wasn't the case
at all; the government was pursuing a case against him because
it had evidence of bribery and bank fraud. However, that didn't
mean that race wasn't on the mind of the U.S. Attorney leading
the prosecution.

Federal prosecutors originally had obtained an indictment
against Ford in 1987 from a grand jury in eastern Tennessee. He
wasn't tried until 1990. That trial, in Memphis, ended in a mis-
trial with the jury deadlocked 8–4, with the eight black members voting to acquit and the four whites voting to convict. In

advance of a retrial, the judge held that an impartial jury could not be found in Ford's hometown, and so ordered that a new jury would be selected from a pool of jurors living eighty miles from Memphis in rural, predominantly white and Republican counties, and then bused into Memphis for the trial. Ford appealed twice, claiming that he was being denied a jury of his peers. The appeals court ruled against him both times.

As the new trial was starting and the jury being selected, I received a request for a meeting from Ford's defense counsel, Bill McDaniels, a nationally respected lawyer whom I had known since law school. Though I didn't know much about the Ford case at the time, I accepted McDaniels's request simply because I had a high regard for him. He had tried other criminal cases in the South and had seen cases where jury selection was manipulated to exploit racial divisions. But he claimed that he had never seen anything like what was happening in the Ford case where, at one point, the prosecutor had struck every black juror in the pool in an apparent attempt to get an all-white jury.

Though the claim was concerning, I didn't take it at face value. Instead, I summoned the U.S. Attorney and the lead prosecutor to Washington to explain the situation. They countered that they simply were striking jurors on the basis of demonstrable bias, not race. I found them unconvincing, believing that they had improperly conflated bias with race. I forced the resignation of the U.S. Attorney when he refused my instruction to go back to court and request that a jury be picked from Memphis itself. Instead, I sent a lawyer from the Criminal Division in Washington to present such a motion to the court.

The result was ironic. Denying the DOJ request, and over

great public outcry, the trial judge seated a jury of eleven whites and one black person. Perhaps in the light of pre-trial publicity or events and discussions concerning race, or simply the way the prosecutor presented the case, the jurors surprisingly went on to acquit Ford of all of the charges against him. Sometimes you try to do your best to obtain justice, but it is the system itself that is self-correcting.

FEDERAL PROSECUTION AS AN ETHICAL UNDERTAKING

The Justice Department bestows the Henry E. Petersen Memorial Award on those who have made a lasting contribution to DOJ's Criminal Division and who exemplify character, diligence, courage, professionalism and talent. There is a good reason for it, and critics on the left and right should take notice of it.

The federal prosecutor owes a special duty to the public and to the court to argue responsibly and always state the facts as they are, not as one might like them to be. If government lawyers were forced to fight with a metaphorical hand tied behind their back, they welcomed the challenge, and more often than not persevered and prevailed.

Prosecutors have great power in their charging decisions and in the conduct of criminal litigation. Their decisions and the results they produce must be "durable." That is, their actions must be perceived as fair and consistent by the public whose members need to know they are expected to conform their conduct to the requirements of the law and, not just to obey the law, but to respect it. And as a result of scrupulous screening and preparation, the government achieves a high conviction rate and most criminal cases result in guilty pleas, with the added outcome that prosecutors' recommendations within the framework of the sentencing guidelines are generally given great weight. This magnifies the prosecutors' responsibility to assure that the sentences of offenders in comparable cases are not made disparate by racial, economic or social bias or personal favoritism.

Adherence to these principles is what caused now more than 2,600 former prosecutors and Department of Justice lawyers to sign a letter of protest concerning the Trump administration's Attorney General's decision to override, apparently without consulting them, the trial team's strategies and sentencing recommendation in the case of individuals who had violated the law in supporting the misconduct of the soon-to-be defeated president. Though he has many attributes, including a keen intellect, that Attorney General had never been a prosecutor. He had never stood before a federal jury and announced, with humility that the United States of America is ready for trial, or allocuted on behalf of the victims at a criminal sentencing. It is not a necessary qualification to be the Attorney General to have done those things, but I can say from my own experience that it helps.

It was reassuring to be among a group of former (and many present) federal prosecutors who were willing to express publicly their condemnation of activities that emitted more of a whiff of favoritism than principle.

Of course, it is not unusual for subordinates to have disputes with line lawyers and to override their recommendations. Indeed, while Acting Attorney General during the Clinton administration, I caused the discharge of two U.S. Attorneys and an FBI Director. But those actions involved disagreements of substance, intended on my part to assure consistency with settled law, not to create disparity in its administration. That is usually the case, irrespective of personalities, politics or policy. Echoing Justice Sutherland, it is the independent federal prosecutor who is at the core of the mechanism that keeps it that way.

When many citizens on the left and on the right, particularly young lawyers planning their careers, are asking whether DOJ stands for the rule of law or for the rule of authoritarian national leaders, adherence to the law and the DOJ's traditions demands that it clearly be the former. There is no room for error or even the perception of it being otherwise. And for those young lawyers, it is a time to step up, not step away.

7

FEC = Feckless Election Commission

by Trevor Potter

Trevor Potter attended Harvard College and the University of Virginia Law School. He is a leading expert on campaign finance and election law as well as ethics in government and served as a Commissioner and Chair of the Federal Election Commission. In this field, we worked together on numerous cases, including the McConnell case discussed in Chapter 1. Trevor has been a partner in the firm of Caplin & Drysdale in Washington, D.C., and is now president of the Campaign Legal Center, a nonpartisan, nonprofit focused on democracy issues. He served in 2000 and 2008 as General Counsel of Senator John McCain's presidential-election campaigns.

The intersection of law and politics is of fundamental importance to our democracy, because what happens at that intersection impacts voter access to the ballot, fair representation in government, ethical standards for government officials, access for eligible voters to participate meaningfully in the democratic process, and voter faith in elected officials. That intersection is where one finds the perennial struggle in our nation to prevent

partisan or special interests from dominating or hijacking our
political system to the detriment of the broader electorate.

I had an opportunity to play a role in this ongoing battle in
1991, when President George H. W. Bush appointed me to the
Federal Election Commission (FEC). Congress created the FEC
in the wake of the Watergate scandal, and it is the only agency
tasked with overseeing the integrity of campaigns for federal
office. Viewed by many in Washington as a career dead end, I
saw a chance to serve at an agency where effective administration
and even-handed enforcement of the law could reduce political
corruption.

I had seen our campaign finance system up close as a lawyer for the presidential campaign of President Bush in 1988. In
that role, I advised the campaign throughout the primaries, the
Republican convention, the general election, the inauguration,
and during the automatic FEC audit of the campaign's spending
activities. There's an old saying that you never want to see how
the sausage gets made. In my case, getting an insider's view of
campaigns, and the failure of the FEC to enforce the campaign
finance laws in a timely manner, only increased my resolve to
play a constructive role in service of a more inclusive, transpar-
ent political process.

Over the next four years, I served in various capacities at the
FEC including as Chairman in 1994. During that time, I strove to
improve agency operations and direct the creation of new campaign finance regulations to further the FEC's mission.

An early opportunity to improve the Commission presented itself when the *Wall Street Journal* published a story about
a corporate whistleblower who had been fired allegedly because

of the employee's objections to the corporation's alleged illegal political activities. It seemed clear that the FEC ought to investigate the allegations. My subsequent discussions with the General Counsel of the Commission, however, revealed that the FEC was not planning on investigating because nobody outside the Commission had filed a complaint regarding the allegations. Seeking to force the question, I filed a complaint myself, which caused a bit of an uproar. The negotiations that followed produced an agreement whereby Commission members could ask the General Counsel to review matters of concern if they were already known to the public, and the Commission would do so if a commissioner from each party signed onto the referral. My judgment about the importance of the case that spurred this change in FEC procedures proved correct, as it eventually resulted in the FEC's assessment of a historic fine.

Over the course of my tenure, I discovered other aspects of the FEC that required attention and amendment. When I arrived, the FEC operated under a "first in, first out" system for handling cases. It made no effort to prioritize consequential matters over those that were trivial. Cases were essentially stacked in a pile with the most recent submission placed on top. Once a procedural action was taken, a case would move down to the bottom of the pile, which had the effect of greatly increasing the timeline for resolving cases. This was not an accident or oversight. Commissioners feared they would be accused of partisanship if they prioritized some matters over others.

I worked with the office of the General Counsel and my colleagues to develop a system that ranked cases for consideration based on non-partisan, objective factors such as how much money was involved, the time-sensitive nature of a given case, the possibility of a case posing novel legal issues, and the potential for a case to be referred to the U.S. Department of Justice for criminal prosecution. FEC staff were given the ability to rate cases as they were submitted.

I also strongly advocated for the creation of what eventually became the equivalent of a traffic-ticket system for dealing with minor infractions of the law such as late campaign-finance filings. Instead of devoting unnecessary resources to low-grade infractions of the law, the traffic-ticket system created a neutral method for assessing fines, resulting in more even-handed enforcement in cases concerning political challengers and incumbents.

Crucial to the FEC's mission is its ability to craft guidelines that help political candidates and others stay within the bounds of the laws passed by Congress. My primary contribution in this area was an effort to create regulations responsive to a George H. W. Bush-era law that expanded the ban on using campaign funds for personal reasons to include all sitting lawmakers. Needless to say, trying to tell members of Congress what they could or could not do with the money they raised did not win me many fans on Capitol Hill. I recall a particularly uncomfortable meeting in the office of the member of Congress who chaired the Oversight Committee. He hated the idea of the FEC creating new rules that would, among other things, govern his wife's use of his campaign's Cadillac in his home district! The pressure to do nothing was keenly felt by my fellow Commission members, who were hesitant to anger the individuals holding the purse strings to the Commission. Nonetheless, new regulations were adopted in 1995, which went into effect later that year. The regulations barred candidates from using campaign funds to pay bills that would have existed whether or not they had run for office. This could include expenses such as home mortgage payments, tuition for family members, club memberships, and tickets to sports events.

Despite the occasional skirmish over issues that challenged the status quo at the FEC, my experience was one of collegiality. To the best of my recollection, we had only a single instance of deadlock in an enforcement matter. Our bipartisan view as commissioners was that the law should be enforced equally on all candidates and committees, with no favoritism shown to either side. My fellow commissioners and I were committed to the notion that laws regulating campaign spending and requiring disclosure were necessary to protect ordinary voters and our democracy.

Since my time at the FEC, and especially over the last decade, things have changed significantly. The story is one of gridlock and dysfunction with 3–3 ties on any issues of importance becoming the norm. This has allowed campaign participants across the political spectrum to break the law with little law enforcement consequences.

Bureaucratic morass and industry capture are not unusual in our nation's capital. The degree of inaction at the FEC, however, is intolerable. As a thought experiment, imagine the Department of Interior refusing to marshal resources to stop the spread of wildfires, or the Food and Drug Administration failing to even discuss approving a vaccine in the face of a deadly virus. The current campaign finance mess does not concern questions of life and death for actual people, but it does pose an existential threat to our system of government. Without a functional FEC, we will never be able to adequately addresses the threat to our democracy, because it is the only government agency tasked with overseeing the integrity of our political campaigns.

The current state of affairs can be tied directly to the FEC's structure, and the refusal of the commissioners to take action, even when faced with overwhelming evidence of unlawful activity. By law, the FEC is made up of six members nominated by the president of the United States and confirmed by the Senate. No more than three of those members are permitted to be affiliated with the same political party. To move anything of substance forward, at least four of the six members must vote in favor. The law essentially requires a bipartisan vote for any Commission action. It is worth noting that this same arrangement existed while I served on the FEC, and yet the Commission voted 3–3 just once during that time, by accident.

As a former Republican commissioner, it gives me no pleasure to point out that it is the Republican commissioners who have routinely refused to deliver votes in pursuit of the rule of law during this period. Their malfeasance seems to be more ideological than partisan, as there have been many cases of alleged violations by Democratic campaigns that have gone nowhere thanks to their intransigence.

To get to the heart of the matter, much of the blame must go to the congressional leaders and political ideologues who impose their agenda by selecting FEC members who are willing to deadlock the Commission rather than lead it on a bipartisan basis. Unable to garner public support for abolishing the Commission altogether, or for revoking campaign finance laws, they achieve their goals by disabling the FEC from within.

This particular quagmire is almost unique among federal

agencies. The FEC is one of only two that is evenly divided along partisan lines, and career FEC staff have less power to take action compared to other agencies. Despite these structural weaknesses, I do not believe the lawmakers who created the FEC had some devious plan to undermine campaign finance enforcement. Deadlocks happened relatively infrequently during the first thirty years of the FEC's existence. The recent stalemate is stunning and unprecedented, causing the FEC to leave its core functions unfulfilled, to the detriment of our democracy.

A casual observer could be forgiven for believing that the FEC's failure to act is restricted to controversial cases or situations where a lack of evidence makes it impossible to proceed. The truth is that the regulatory process at today's FEC is routinely short-circuited, with many complaints getting stuck in the preliminary stage of examination, despite credible evidence of wrongdoing. When a complaint is filed, the accused have an opportunity to respond, and the FEC's General Counsel compiles an analysis. Commissioners then vote on whether or not to open a formal investigation, known in agency jargon as finding "reason to believe" enough information has been presented to probe deeper into a complaint. All too often, deadlocks occur at this stage of the process, and the agency has no option but to drop the case. Opponents of campaign finance regulation have pointed to these tied early-stage votes as evidence of the FEC ruling on the merits of a given complaint, a disingenuous interpretation of agency procedures conjured up to justify an ideological predisposition towards inaction.

There is ample evidence of the Commission's recent paralysis. The FEC admitted to Congress in 2019 that it had at least one deadlocked vote in the majority (51 percent) of the enforcement matters considered since 2012.

The deadlocking problem goes well beyond the agency's unwillingness to investigate credible allegations. The trend is also notable by its impact on the FEC's role in providing crucial guidance to campaigns and other entities. FEC "advisory opinions" are issued in response to requests from political actors and provide clarification about existing law. Even this seemingly straightforward task has been hampered by gridlock, with an analysis by the Brennan Center for Justice finding the rate at which the commissioners fail to agree on how to respond to requests for guidance, increasing more than fivefold in recent years.

The Commission has also fallen down on the job when it comes to updating its regulations and issuing new rules to account for changes in the campaign finance landscape brought on by court rulings and other developments. This is important because the FEC is charged with adopting regulations that implement the campaign finance law passed by Congress, and failing to do so risks allowing these laws to become dangerously out of date. For instance, the FEC has failed to adopt a single substantive regulation regarding the so-called "super PACs" which it is empowered to do under the Federal Election Campaign Act (FECA) of 1971. Meanwhile, these vehicles have been used to spend billions of dollars, including vast sums by wealthy individuals and corporations, to influence elections over the past decade.

The timing of this precipitous regulatory decline could not be worse, as it has coincided with (and helped drive) an immense surge in campaign spending that should be the subject of ongoing scrutiny. An estimated $14.4 billion was spent during the presidential and congressional campaigns in 2020 alone, compared to just $598 million in 1980. The avenues through which this torrent of cash flows have utterly blurred the lines that are supposed to exist between candidates and outside special interests. Raising money for one purpose, then turning around and using that money for a campaign that is not allowed to use such funds? No problem. Outside interests funneling money through multiple front groups to disguise the true source and size of their contributions? Go ahead. Campaigns working hand in glove with outside groups that are technically banned from coordinating with each other? No worries say the Republicans on the FEC who deny the agency the opportunity to investigate and sanction wrongdoing.

The FEC's track record of inaction, driven by the ideology of its Republican members who exploit the agency's structure, is particularly visible on the issues of disclosure and coordination. On both fronts, the FEC could be making significant progress for the good of our democracy, but that remains a pipe dream.

The Supreme Court's mistaken 2010 ruling in *Citizens United* opened the door for unlimited election-related spending by corporations, otherwise known as "independent expenditures." The majority opinion, written by Justice Anthony Kennedy, asserted that "citizens can see whether elected officials are 'in the pocket' of so-called moneyed interests" and disclosure will "enable the electorate to make informed decisions and give proper weight to different speakers and messages." Despite this clear direction from the court, the FEC has failed to update its disclosure rules to account for the post-*Citizens United* environment.

Indeed, since *Citizens United* was decided, it has become commonplace to see special interests, including both wealthy individuals and corporations, unlawfully funnel their election spending through obscurely-named limited liability companies (LLCs), trusts, or other "straw donor" entities to avoid public disclosure of the true contributors' identities, thereby effectively denying voters the ability to "make informed decisions" as Justice Kennedy had naively forecast.

Because the FEC has by and large failed to enforce the laws that have long prohibited these kinds of "straw donor" contribution schemes, it bears a significant share of the blame for what even Justice Kennedy acknowledged five years after *Citizens United*: that the disclosure he had envisioned was not "working the way it should."

Soon after *Citizens United*, the Court of Appeals for the District of Columbia Circuit in *speechnow.org v. FEC*, ruled against limits on independent expenditures because, by their very nature, they would not cause corruption. This decision led to the creation of super PACs, political committees that can raise and spend unlimited amounts from individuals, corporations, and unions, as long as they only use those funds to make independent expenditures, i.e., they do not coordinate their election spending with the candidates they are supporting.

Once again, anti-regulation dogma has stymied efforts to enforce coordination restrictions. In 2019, the agency admitted to Congress that it had not, as of that time, found a single violation of its rules on coordination since *Citizen's United*. This is not due to a lack of clear, public evidence of coordination presented to the FEC. Instead, the Commission has repeatedly deadlocked on whether to even permit an investigation or has failed to vote at all.

The FEC's failures are not limited to allegations against supporters of Republican candidates. One of the FEC's more egregious failures to address disclosure and coordination concerns the 2016 presidential campaign of Hillary Clinton.

While the challenges that prevent the FEC from functioning properly are formidable, a host of solutions are available to remedy the current impasse. I would suggest that politicians who have the power to enact such changes pay heed to survey after survey finding that the vast majority of American voters across the political spectrum are unhappy with the current campaign finance system and want reform.

In an ideal world, there would be a return to the "good old days," when Commission appointees representing the two major political parties believed in the FEC's mission and acted accordingly. In the absence of such a eureka moment, legislative fixes must be considered. The most widely discussed proposals would end the ability of less than a majority of commissioners to block the FEC's professional lawyers and investigators from doing their jobs; change the number of commissioners from six to five to avoid deadlocks; or depoliticize the nomination process by creating a nonpartisan panel that recommends nominees to the president.

One proposal I find particularly appealing is changing federal law so that four votes would be required to reject a recommendation by the FEC's General Counsel to investigate allegations of unlawful activity, rather than requiring four votes to approve the professional staff's recommendation. This might be

coupled with a statutory time limit during which the bloc opposing the staff recommendations would have to act. Under such a
system, the FEC's General Counsel and other nonpartisan, non-
political enforcement staff would still be required to follow the
enforcement procedures already established by law and enforcement policies previously approved by the Commission. Legislation has been introduced in previous Congresses that would
require this change. However, as with so many pro-democracy
bills of late, the Freedom to Vote Act did not make it past a
Republican-led filibuster in the Senate.

A failure to reform the FEC, either by its own hand or by
statute, will continue to exact an unacceptable toll on our elec-
toral process. Open coordination between candidates and super-
PACs continues to evolve, becoming worse and more flagrant. A
fairly recent example of this was the Trump campaign in 2019
sending an email telling supporters that "There is one approved
outside non-campaign group, America First Action, which is run
by allies of the president, and is a trusted supporter of President
Trump's policies and agendas." Politicians on both sides of the
aisle have increasingly adopted a blatantly illegal practice known
as "redboxing" in which campaigns post detailed instructions for
desired election ads on a website for outside groups to follow,
and in some cases even supply material for such ads, including
as downloadable stock pictures of the candidate and b-roll video.

Later on, I became deeply involved in a bipartisan effort
by Arizona Senator John McCain and Wisconsin Senator Russ
Feingold to address glaring weaknesses in our campaign finance
law. The bill, which eventually came to be known as the Bipartisan Campaign Reform Act (BCRA), sought to prohibit political

parties from raising unlimited sums of money via donations from corporate and labor interests or wealthy donors ("soft money"). The Senators also wanted to restrict certain types of political ads paid for by corporations and unions since they were already prohibited from participating in federal election advocacy. I was part of a working group, which collaborated with constitutional law experts to create a bill that would withstand likely court challenges.

BCRA was signed into law in 2002, and for a brief period, I hoped we were on a path toward reining in the excesses of our campaign finance system. Much to my dismay, however, the FEC repeatedly failed to enforce the new law, and despite withstanding a legal challenge in *McConnell v. U.S.* in 2003 (discussed in more detail in the first essay of this volume), the Supreme Court's subsequent rulings, including *Citizens United,* dashed any hope that the law could live up to the expectations of its backers. Campaign Legal Center, which I founded in 2002, repeatedly challenged flawed FEC regulations in court, and won. But the FEC either wrote new equally flawed rules, or simply continued to fail to enforce the law.

The degree to which secret spending has come to dominate our political system since these events is simply astounding. Billions have been spent over the last few election cycles, in an ever-increasing flow of unaccountable campaign cash. This breakdown of the rule of law is deeply disturbing on its own, but it is occurring in concert with profoundly dangerous trends that are severely undermining our democracy.

The pursuit of self-government of, by, and for the people depends on creating and nurturing a political process that empowers ordinary voters. Our distorted, dysfunctional campaign finance system has the opposite effect because it allows powerful special interests to rig the system in their favor and deprives voters of their right to know who is spending, to influence their decisions in the voting booth. This toxic environment is further polluted by a redistricting process that in many states essentially allows politicians to choose their voters, the opposite of how our system is supposed to operate. Add to the stew a corrosive, conspiracy-driven ideology that seeks to cast doubt on our election outcomes, and a political class on the right side of the spectrum that is content to exploit that ideology for the purpose of maintaining power, primarily through restricting the freedom to vote.

Combating these ills has occupied the bulk of my professional career. During this period, I have learned that persistence is the best course of action in the face of rising threats to our democracy. That is why, despite the seemingly intractable state of the agency I used to manage, I, along with my colleagues at Campaign Legal Center, will continue to press for progress whenever the opportunity arises.

SECTION II

PEOPLE

8

Prelude to a Massacre

by Roger M. Witten

Archibald Cox was a Yankee born and bred. He was schooled at St. Paul's, Harvard College, and Harvard Law School. He joined the Harvard Law faculty and taught labor law and constitutional law. Cox had close-cropped hair and wore bow ties. His somewhat chirpy voice resonated with a finely-honed New England aristocratic accent.

Cox was no stranger to Washington, D.C. Nominated by President Kennedy, Cox served as Solicitor General—the third ranking officer in the Department of Justice and the U.S. Government's advocate in the Supreme Court.

In June of 1972, a bungled burglary at the Democratic National Committee headquarters at the Watergate apartment complex set into motion a series of events that plunged the country into crisis. As time passed and more evidence came to light, it appeared possible that the White House had orchestrated or supported a cover-up of evidence connecting the burglars to President Richard Nixon's reelection committee and to the White House.

Pressure mounted for the appointment by Attorney General Elliot Richardson of a special prosecutor who would conduct an independent criminal grand jury investigation into the allegations of a cover-up. Richardson was also a Yankee aristocrat and a long-time friend of Cox. Archibald Cox, however, was not Richardson's first choice for the job. Indeed, Richardson's papers indicate that he approached seven other people before turning to Cox. When asked, Cox agreed to serve. Cox quickly set out to build what became known as the Watergate Special Prosecution Force (WSPF) on which I served.

On July 16, 1973, a White House aide, Alexander Butterfield, shocked the Nation when he disclosed to a congressional investigative committee that, at President Nixon's request, a secret taping system had been installed in the Oval Office. It was immediately recognized that the tapes might reveal powerful evidence bearing on whether a crime had been committed.

Thus began a drawn-out drama. After the White House failed to cooperate by producing the tapes to the WSPF, Cox sent subpoenas to the White House demanding production of eight (later nine) tape-recording excerpts of conversations on specific dates and at specific times which were potentially relevant according to testimony given by White House aides. The White House declined to comply, citing Executive Privilege among other points. Thereafter, District Court Judge John Sirica rejected the White House's objections, as did the Court of Appeals for the District of Columbia Circuit.

Skipping over many intervening developments, suffice it to say the final battle lines were drawn when the White House insisted on the so-called "Stennis Compromise." The notion was that Stennis, who was a superannuated and rather deaf segregationist Mississippi Senator, would listen to the tapes and make judgments about relevancy and privilege. In addition, the "compromise" would have required Cox to agree that the WSPF would only receive summaries of the tapes, not the actual tapes, and that the WSPF would also agree that it would not request any additional tapes going forward.

The tension peaked when Cox indicated that he could not agree to the White House proposal and the White House let it be known that it would fire Cox if he did not relent.

Cox held a press conference on Saturday morning, October 20, that was televised and broadcast live nationwide. Cox thought that because his refusal to assent to this "compromise" might further plunge the country into crisis, he owed it to American citizens to explain his reasoning. He also wanted to make it costly for the President to order that he be fired.

In the WSPF office, there was concern about how Cox would relate to ordinary Americans—here was this professorial, bow-tie-wearing New England icon who dazzled in classrooms and courtrooms, but would he "play in Peoria."

The press conference was packed with WSPF staff, the press, and others, while millions watched on TV. Cox entered the room, holding hands with his wife Phyllis, and wearing a normal tie. And then he spoke to America.

He didn't deliver a law lecture and he didn't use "fighting words." Indeed, he didn't sound at all like he was arguing a case. Rather he acted and sounded like a modest public servant who felt he had a duty to explain himself, and he did so in plain, sometimes folksy, English.

After apologizing for bringing people in on a beautiful weekend morning, he pointed to a newspaper headline "Cox defiant." He then demurred: "I must say I don't feel defiant . . . I'm not looking for a confrontation . . . I'm even worried that I'm getting too big for my britches, that what I see as principle could be vanity. I hope not . . . In the end I decided I had to try to stick by what I thought was right." He then walked through what he thought was right.

He first explained why he thought he had a duty to pursue the tapes: "It appears that the papers, documents and recordings of conversations in the White House, including the tapes, would be relevant to getting the truth about these incidents . . . I think it is my duty as the special prosecutor, as an officer of the court and as the representative of the grand jury, to bring to the court's attention what seems to me to be noncompliance with the court's order."

Cox next explained why it was important to pursue this evidence in this particular situation: "when criminal wrongdoing is the subject of investigation, and when one of those subjects is obstruction of justice in the form of a cover-up, then it seems to me it is simply not enough to make a compromise in which the real evidence is available only to two or three men operating in secrecy, all but one of them aides to the President and men who have been associated with those who are the subject of the investigation . . . it's the kind of question where it is terribly important to adhere to the established institutions and not to accommodate it by some private arrangement involving, as I say, submitting the evidence ultimately to any one man." He then made the practical point: "It's most unlikely . . . that a summary of the tapes would be admissible in evidence."

Cox said he had concluded that he could not accede to the White House demands without violating the oath he had given the Senate.

Almost instantaneously, supporting telegrams and other messages began pouring into the WSPF office. What Cox succeeded in doing was to convince a jury composed of millions of Americans that he was a man of integrity and sincerity—a decent man whose judgment inspired confidence. He moved a nation.

The victory was costly. That same night, the Solicitor General, Robert Bork, executed President Nixon's order to fire Cox, which Attorney General Richardson and Deputy Attorney General William Ruckelshaus had declined to do. The ensuing criticisms of the "Saturday Night Massacre" however made it impossible as a practical matter for the White House to carry out its plan to fire the entire WSPF staff. As is said, the rest is history.

• • •

Working on the WSPF was an incredible experience for a young lawyer. How I got the job is a good story too.

In my second year at Harvard Law School, I took Archibald Cox's constitutional law class. He gave the class the option of writing three papers jointly with a classmate in lieu of taking exams. My dear friend Jim Quarles and I decided to take that option and to write the papers together. To everyone's surprise, our first paper earned the highest grade in the class. As did our second and third papers. Then in our third year, we did well in Cox's constitutional law seminar. Long story short—we knew Cox and he knew us.

In those days, some federal judges essentially outsourced their law clerk selection process to distinguished professors. Cox tapped me to clerk for Judge Harrison Winter, a highly regarded jurist who sat on the Fourth Circuit Court of Appeals in Baltimore (coincidently, Jim had already secured a clerkship with Judge Frank Kaufman, who was a noted district court judge in Baltimore).

Fast forward to May 1973 when Cox is appointed to be the Watergate special prosecutor. Jim and I seriously considered making an effort to apply to join Cox's team, but we were not comfortable with the notion of leaving our clerkships early and so, after agonizing over a weekend, we decided to stay put.

When Judge Winter arrived in chambers the next morning, he asked me to come to his office. After morning pleasantries, he said he had read of Cox's appointment in the newspapers and he was sure Cox would need some junior lawyers. He went on to say that, were he a young lawyer, he would have aspired to such a job, and if I had such aspirations, he would write to Cox to recommend that Cox hire me—immediately. About a week later, I joined the WSPF staff.

And Jim? Judge Kaufman was not quite as selfless as Judge Winter. But about three months later, he freed Jim to join the WSPF.

9

Resilience

by Andrew Tannenbaum

Andrew Tannenbaum graduated from Dartmouth College and Columbia Law School. He clerked for Judge Wilfred Feinberg on the U.S. Court of Appeals for the Second Circuit in New York and writes about the Judge here. Thereafter, he has worked at the Department of Justice, National Security Agency, IBM, and Barclays. He is my son-in-law.

On September 11, 2001, Judge Wilfred Feinberg was preparing for his usual morning walk from his apartment in Battery Park City to the federal courthouse at Foley Square in downtown Manhattan. Appointed thirty-five years earlier by President Lyndon Johnson to the U.S. Court of Appeals for the Second Circuit, Judge Feinberg had made this same trip by foot countless times. He enjoyed living near the courthouse and had grown quite fond of his daily stroll and the city sights along the way. Had he left his building that morning, the twenty-minute commute would have taken him within mere feet of the most visible and impressive structure in the neighborhood—the World Trade Center.

That morning, the Second Circuit was scheduled to hear

oral arguments in its first cases for the 2001–2002 term. Just two weeks earlier, I had started a one-year clerkship in Judge Feinberg's chambers. It had been an intense and awe-inspiring learning period, getting to know the judge and preparing bench memos for each case. At this, the start of my legal career, I was eager to dive into the work of the court. With the first hearings suddenly upon us, September 11 felt like a special day. Filled with anticipation, with the *Today Show* playing in the background, I put on my favorite red tie—a distinct visual etched in my memory. Needless to say, neither the judge nor I made it to the courthouse that day.

Like many New Yorkers, Judge Feinberg and his wife Shirley found themselves walking north, away from the burning towers. They traipsed up the West Side Highway, along the Hudson River without a clear destination or way to get there. At eighty-one years old, the judge could have been forgiven for finding that trek daunting. But he was still a pretty decent walker, as evidenced by his daily mile-long journey to and from the courthouse. And Shirley, six years his junior, was known for her boundless energy. In their rush to vacate, they had left all their belongings behind and the windows in their apartment wide open (it was a beautiful September morning and Shirley loved the cool, fresh air). After many failed attempts at hailing a ride, they finally convinced a taxi filling up at a gas station to take them to a friend's place on the Upper East Side.

With uncertainty, fear, and dust in the air, I escaped the city that night on a train from Grand Central to my parents' house in New Rochelle. The iconic station was eerily deserted, yet it felt like a target. We moved through it quickly and nervously.

The train conductor, with an unforgettable look of weariness and disbelief, refused to take any payment for tickets.

The next day, safely ensconced in the suburbs, I took a long walk with Wendy, my wife of four months. The conversation was emotional, as the reality and scale of the human loss caught up with us. We had also been law school classmates, and we pondered what this catastrophic event would mean for the direction of law and policy in America.

Over the next two days, Judge Feinberg and I were trying to get in touch. I'm not sure how he tracked me down without access to his Rolodex, but I soon received a message on my answering machine, "Andrew, this is the Judge."

He had a booming, deep voice—legendarily deep, actually—and it filled our Murray Hill one-bedroom as if he were handing down a ruling in the living room. I was relieved to hear from him, and he told me of the court's arrangements to carry on with judicial business. The plan was that the law clerks for all the Second Circuit judges were going to be driven to the courthouse to pick up the case files. The hearings would be rescheduled at an alternate location. And I would be escorted to the Feinbergs' apartment to pick up medicines and other personal items (this took some convincing of the judge, but eventually he agreed).

Back at Grand Central, I waited on the corner of Lexington Avenue with the other law clerks for our journey downtown. Our ride turned out to be a New York City Department of Corrections bus, used in normal times to transport prisoners. Sitting in the place of inmates was unexpectedly jarring and added to the already unsettling feel of the trip. It was not lost on any of us that we were headed into a completely closed off area of Lower

Manhattan, blocks from Ground Zero, mere days after the attack. We took a hauntingly empty FDR Parkway south along the East River, avoiding the World Trade Center site to the southwest.

The first thing you noticed was the smell. Anyone who was down there during the aftermath remembers it—metallic, burning toxicity. It would linger for months, but we didn't have much time to dwell on it that day as we headed up the elevators to our respective judges' chambers.

I entered Judge Feinberg's office—a roomy space that was both dignified and humble, like the man himself. He took particular pride in his office because its immediate prior occupant was none other than Thurgood Marshall, whom Judge Feinberg succeeded in 1966 (and for whom the courthouse itself had just been ceremoniously named in August 2001). Justice Marshall's oversized dictionary, which my co-clerk and I relished using when the occasion struck, was displayed on a pedestal next to Judge Feinberg's desk. An adjacent bookcase along the wall comprised Judge Feinberg's system for organizing cases: rows of magazine file boxes, each meticulously positioned and labeled by pending case, containing the parties' briefs and our internal legal research. Like the worn rug and furniture, this same system had been in place for decades. I grabbed the papers for the upcoming oral arguments and headed downstairs.

My next mission was not as simple. In the courthouse lobby, I met two U.S. Marshals. One of them handed me an FBI windbreaker. I paused for a second, wondering if impersonating a federal law enforcement officer was the best move for a brand-new lawyer. Sensing my hesitation, they told me that if anyone asked if I was actually FBI, to keep moving and not look back. Who was

I to argue? I put on the jacket, and we started on our walk to the Feinbergs' apartment in Battery City Park. Clearly, I did not look the part, and when we were gently questioned at the very first (and only) checkpoint, I immediately started stammering. The Marshals rolled their eyes, gave me a disappointed smile, and hurried me along.

The hellscape we came upon was unimaginable. Shards of the buildings pierced through piles of rubble. There was a UPS truck completely flattened like a pancake. Everything seemed upside down. Through the chaos and haze, official delegations were inspecting the wreckage. Mayor Rudy Guiliani and Senator Hillary Clinton, almost as unlikely a pair then as they would be now, walked together, right past us.

I had completely lost my sense of direction, but the Marshals navigated us to Judge Feinberg's building. All we had to do was go up to his twenty-third-floor apartment and retrieve a short list of items. But . . . there was no power in the building and it had not yet been deemed safe to occupy. We had heard that airplane parts were impaled in the exterior walls. And there were rumors of other buildings nearby being unstable and at risk of collapsing.

We had flashlights and surgical masks (not N95s), and we took it slow. As we climbed the narrow flights, with heavy breath and beading sweat, it was impossible not to picture those who found themselves in stairwells of the burning towers just days earlier. Even though I had fully volunteered for this assignment, and even though objectively we were not in any danger, moments of real panic crept in. The Marshals were amazing, keeping us moving up the steps with welcome humor about who was in worse physical shape. When we finally reached the twenty-third floor, we found a lovely apartment with windows wide open, covered in a thick layer of dust.

We didn't talk as much about resilience back then as we do now, but resilience was on display everywhere that year—including the federal courts. Despite the severe disruption to the city, the oral arguments that were cancelled on September 11 were held the very next week in an extraordinary session at the New York City Bar Association in mid-town. On September 24, less than two weeks after the attacks, hearings resumed at the courthouse itself. The environment and mood had changed—there were now armed guards with menacing assault weapons stationed around the courthouse perimeter—but the wheels of justice kept turning. This happened without modern communication tools like Zoom, social media, or even texting, and notwithstanding a massive burning pile of debris down the street.

As for the Feinbergs, they took their displacement in remarkable stride. Shirley, who had her own business as a personal fashion shopper, replenished their inaccessible wardrobe. With the help of insurance, they secured an extended-stay hotel room, where they lived for several months. It was not walking distance to the courthouse, but Judge Feinberg quickly adapted to his new commute. He came to work every day with the same unflappable, positive disposition.

They did miss the hubbub of Battery Park City, especially Shirley. She particularly missed her outdoor plot in the community garden, which she had helped establish years earlier. Smothered by ash and with dislocated caretakers, the plants were at risk. As soon as she was allowed, Shirley returned to the garden and spent hours cleaning the plants and restoring the plots. Months later, she took me there and proudly showed off the progress. It was as if she had been rebuilding Battery Park City with her own hands.

The most enduring memories from the remaining months of my clerkship were those forged around the dining table in Judge Feinberg's office during weekly one-on-one lunches. There was much going on in the world to talk about, and it was fascinating to hear his take on these major events. He had seen a lot in his time—from being deployed in World War II as an Army intelligence officer, to being nominated to a federal district court seat by President Kennedy, to serving as Chief Judge of the Second Circuit for eight years. He had written seminal wartime opinions, upholding a Vietnam War-era law that prohibited the burning of draft cards, and dissenting from a decision that would have delayed the publication of the Pentagon Papers in the *New York Times* (his position was vindicated days later when the Supreme Court allowed the publication to go forward). As the different positions in those cases suggest, he had both a deep concern for civil liberties and profound respect for military service. He was certainly drawing on that experience as he assessed America's response to 9/11.

At one of our lunches, Judge Feinberg told me about a harrowing experience he had during World War II. He was a skilled codebreaker and was deployed on the USS *Orizaba* in 1943 as part of a large convoy involved in the Allied invasion of Sicily. Soon after its arrival off the coast of Sicily, his ship was bombed in an enemy air attack. Fortunately, Feinberg was on the side of the ship that was not bombed, but he lost friends on the other side. When I asked him how he made it through such a frightening event, he told me that he learned not to fear what he could not control. That wisdom felt highly relevant given the anxious state that permeated New York at the time, and it has stuck with me through the years.

We also shared lighter interests. We were both big Yankees fans, and we talked a lot about the team that year, especially during the dramatic 2001 World Series that served as a much-needed catharsis for New York. The judge amazed me when he described seeing Babe Ruth play at Yankee Stadium, and I wowed him with an early version of MLB Gameday as we both followed a live-game pitch-by-pitch on my desktop one afternoon. Improbably, we also shared a love for Camp Scatico, a sleep-away camp we had both attended as campers and counselors over fifty years apart. Legend has it that the judge left standing orders to put through any phone calls from people asking for "Billy" as they must have been camp friends.

As my clerkship wound down, I made plans to move to Washington, D.C. to start a job at the Department of Justice. Judge Feinberg was very supportive, although he did offer words of caution about Washington being a "company town." He was commenting on the possible one-dimensional feel of living in a city where one industry (the government) dominates the job market and cocktail banter. Looking back, I believe he meant this less as a slight to D.C. than he did as a statement about the richness of living in New York. And it occurs to me now that he was subtly, but steadfastly advocating for life in New York after experiencing one of the most trying years in the city's history. He and Shirley were proud New Yorkers, and their love for the city was strengthened, not diminished, by the tragedy of 2001.

The Feinbergs stayed in touch, following my career and growing family like doting grandparents, as they did with all his clerks. Communication with the judge inevitably faded in his later years. Judge Feinberg died in 2014 at age ninety-four, and Shirley died one year later. But the memory of my time with them, and the example that they set, remains strong. To this day, when I encounter a challenging personal moment, or when world events have again taken a frightening turn, I often think of the Feinbergs and take comfort in their wisdom, decency, warmth, and yes, resilience.[1]

1. With special thanks to Judge and Shirley Feinberg's adult children—Jessica Twedt, Susan Stelk, and Jack Feinberg—for sharing their memories of their parents' 9/11 experience.

10

You Win Some and . . .

by James L. Quarles

James Quarles attended Denison University and Harvard Law School where we met and became friends. Jim clerked for Judge Frank Kaufman in Baltimore (at the same time, I was clerking in the same courthouse for another judge). Jim served with me and other contributors to this volume as an Assistant Watergate Special Prosecutor. Following that, Jim joined Hale and Dorr in Boston and later became head of that firm's D. C. office. We became partners when our firms merged. Jim specialized in trial work, and was a leading intellectual property litigation lawyer. Jim served as Senior Counselor to the Special Counsel Robert Mueller (making Jim the only person who served on both the Cox and Mueller teams).

When my time on the Watergate Special Prosecution Force was over, I rented a U-Haul truck, loaded my two-year-old daughter, Jessica, and my pregnant wife, Sharon, and headed to Boston. There never was any doubt I would be heading to Boston to join what was then Hale and Dorr. I had been a summer associate there after my third year of law school and loved Boston.

But even more important were the events of the Saturday

Night Massacre. When Archibald Cox—the constitutional law professor whose classes Roger Witten and I took together—was fired for demanding access to the White House tapes, news reports got one thing dead wrong. A *New York Times* banner headline inaccurately reported "Nixon . . . Abolishes Watergate Task Force." In fact, Robert Bork's letter implementing President Nixon's orders had only fired Archie, not the rest of us.

As we sat around debating whether we should resign in protest, one person asked "Who's going to pay for Quarles's kid to get born?" That same night, I received a call from a partner at Hale and Dorr who said "I know Sharon is pregnant. Don't know whether we can do it, but if you need a job, we will try to get you onto our insurance plan." That, I concluded, was all I needed to know to make up my mind.

When I arrived at Hale and Dorr one of the most prominent lawyers there was James St. Clair, with whom I had worked as a summer associate, and who had for a period represented President Nixon in the Watergate investigation. Jim had a reputation that was larger than life—so large that if Garrett Graff's book *Watergate Revisited* is to be believed, Archie had offered Jim the job of Deputy Watergate Special Prosecutor. In a sign of how less polarized the times were, it didn't seem odd at all that I would be joining a firm with the most visible lawyer on the other side of our office's most visible case.

It wasn't long before Jim asked me to join him on a case. As in most war stories old lawyers tell, the actual facts aren't that relevant. But the case was a criminal case involving the owner of a Chevrolet dealership in Lowell, Massachusetts. After a warranty audit revealed, among other things, that Chevrolet had been charged for the installation of at least five times as many replacement engines as Chevrolet had delivered to the dealership, GM's warranty inspector was found dead in the Danvers River.

Suspicion immediately focused on the service manager, George F. Edgerly. That might well be explained by the fact that in 1959, Edgerly had been accused of dismembering his wife and disposing of her in the Merrimack River. However, represented by a young F. Lee Bailey—who would go on to represent Patty Hearst and O. J. Simpson—Edgerly was acquitted. Suspicion turned to indictment after Edgerly stabbed and nearly killed a co-employee who had threatened to expose Edgerly's murder of the warranty inspector.

Our client, the owner of the dealership, was indicted for warranty fraud along with the company president, and Edgerly. Edgerly was separately indicted for the murder of the warranty inspector. The entire set of facts received so much publicity that the trial was transferred to Leominster, Massachusetts—about an hour and a half west of Boston.

When it came time for trial, Jim decided that he and I would be the only lawyers at the trial representing our client. Each morning we drove an hour and a half to Leominster, talking about what was going to happen that day, and drove home talking about what had happened that day. During the entire time—and the next twenty years we practiced together—Jim never mentioned Watergate. He told great stories about the Army-McCarthy hearings (he was part of the "have you no sense of decency" team), but never a word about Watergate.

Jim had plenty of advice. I was driving a 1966 Volkswagen my father-in-law donated to me while I was in law school. It had been through a lot of tough New England winters and was on its second engine. I typically drove to Jim's house in the morning, and we drove to Leominster in his car. The VW was left in front of Jim's house. On one of those mornings, Jim said "Jimmy, you know it is important for a lawyer to look prosperous so clients will be comfortable that you know what you are doing." I dutifully said "yes."

The next morning, Jim returned to the theme, telling me, "you know I bought a Cadillac when I was a young associate to convey that I was successful." Able to read headlines if not able to get the nuances, I figured this might be a comment on my VW. When Jim brought the issue up a third time, I said, "Jim, I just got out of a low-paying government job, Sharon just had our second child, we just bought a house, and this VW is going to have to last for several years." Jim paused, nodded, and said, "I understand. But my wife has bridge club tomorrow, so could you not park it in front of our house!"

Jim was the consummate trial lawyer. Early in the case Jim said to me, "remember the first rule of being a trial lawyer." I thought, This is exactly why I came back to Hale and Dorr. Jim then deadpanned, "Never miss a chance to go to the bathroom."

Before the trial started, an important issue arose about a case that had been decided the previous week by Massachusetts' highest court. The courtroom was packed with reporters. With the chutzpah that only a third-year lawyer could summon, I said to him, "I read that case, do you want me to argue it?" Jim calmly said "Yes, into my ear."

The case produced a smorgasbord of war stories. Because of the publicity, the jury was going to be sequestered for four to six weeks. The judge asked the potential jurors whether it would be a problem for them to be confined to a hotel for four to six weeks. One of the potential jurors who raised his hand was a large gentleman in overalls. When asked at the podium why he raised his hand, he replied with a thick New England accent, "It wouldn't be a problem for me, but it would be hell on the cows."

As the trial progressed, it became apparent that the service manager had concluded he was likely to be convicted of the murder in the separate trial. After all, he had failed to kill his co-employee who was going to testify against him. And, for good measure, in the interim he had been indicted for rape in one of future Senator John Kerry's first major cases. Edgerly rightly concluded that the warranty fraud claims were the least of his worries. Proving the wisdom of Jim's frequent lament, "Lord save me from co-counsel and co-defendants," Edgerly discharged his lawyer and set about making sure that his co-defendants on the warranty fraud claim were convicted as well. (There never was a suggestion that anyone other than the service manager had anything to do with the murder.) That allowed Edgerly to avoid testifying but to conduct cross-examinations along the lines of "do you remember the time I walked into your office, you were watching the Celtics, and I told you it was a good day because we just hit GM for five new engines?" Go ahead—think of a good answer for your client to give to that question.

But that produced another great Jim lesson: never let them see you sweat. Jim preached that someone on the jury was likely to be watching you at all times. Accordingly, no matter what was going on in the courtroom, Jim's demeanor never changed. Unfailingly polite, the worst testimony imaginable or the worst judicial ruling since Dred Scott never evoked a grimace or head shake. The greatest testimony might—just might—provoke the slightest uptick at the corner of his mouth.

At the conclusion of six weeks of daily commutes and long days in court, Jim delivered his closing argument and we finally could have a meal more formal than a sandwich. But Christmas Eve was the next day and the jury had been sequestered long enough. The jury returned its verdict that same afternoon—guilty. Our client and the president of the dealership were sentenced to two years. Appeals were unsuccessful. Edgerly was sentenced to three years for the warranty fraud, and life in the murder trial. He died in prison.

With his trademark ability to move on, Jim was confident that he could not have done anything better—and he was right—so he was able to say, "next case." That's one lesson Jim could never teach me—for me, it has been "win for a week, lose for a lifetime," meaning you enjoy a win for a week, but remember the losses forever. But the other thing you could do for a lifetime was to learn from Jim.

11

Litigating a High-Profile Criminal Case

by N. Richard Janis

N. Richard ("Dick") Janis graduated from the University of Wisconsin and the Harvard Law School. He is a nationally recognized expert in white collar criminal defense, often involving public figures. He began his career as an Assistant United States Attorney in Washington, D.C. In private practice, he co-founded the firm of Janis, Schuelke, and Wechsler, a highly regarded boutique firm. I met Dick at Harvard, we took the bar exam together, and we worked together on several cases.

ALBERT HAKIM

In 1987, I represented Albert Hakim in the Iran-Contra case. Mr. Hakim was an Iranian-American businessman who ran the web of Swiss companies and bank accounts that were used by National Security Council (NSC) officials John Poindexter and Oliver North to fund the top-secret initiatives undertaken on behalf of the Reagan Administration to support the Contra insurgency in Nicaragua, and to negotiate the release of American hostages being held in Iran. Mr. Hakim also served as a translator in secret talks with Iranian representatives, and was credited for personally negotiating the release of one of the hostages, David Jacobsen.

Shortly after the revelation of the Iran-Contra secret initiatives, an independent counsel, Lawrence Walsh, and a joint House and Senate Select Congressional Committee were appointed to investigate the matter. Mr. Hakim became a principal subject of both investigations. Given Mr. Hakim's status as a private citizen, and what I believed were the political issues that outweighed the importance of a criminal prosecution, I determined that Mr. Hakim would cooperate with both investigations only in return for a grant of immunity under 18 USC Section 6002, which provides:

> Whenever a witness refuses, on the basis of his privilege against self-incrimination, to testify or provide other information in a proceeding before or ancillary to—
>
> (1) a court or grand jury of the United States,
>
> (2) an agency of the United States, or
>
> (3) either House of Congress, a joint committee of the two Houses, or a committee or a subcommittee of either House, and the person presiding over the proceeding communicates to the witness an order issued under this title, the witness may not refuse to comply with the order on the basis of his privilege against self-incrimination; but no testimony or other information compelled under the order (or any information directly or indirectly derived from such testimony or other information) may be used against the witness in any criminal case, except a prosecution for perjury,

giving a false statement, or otherwise failing to comply with the order.

A separate statutory provision made clear that Congress has the power to grant immunity, regardless of the position of the Department of Justice on the matter. 18 USC Section 6005.

The Supreme Court upheld the immunity statutes in *Kastigar v. United States*, 406 U.S. 441 (1972). In so doing, the Court underscored the prohibition against the government's direct or even indirect (derivative) use of immunized testimony in a prosecution of the witness. The Court reaffirmed the burden of proof that must be borne by the government to establish that its evidence is based on independent, legitimate sources:

> This burden of proof, which we affirm as appropriate, is not limited to a negation of taint; rather, it imposes on the prosecution the affirmative duty to prove that the evidence it proposes to use is derived from a legitimate source wholly independent of the compelled testimony. *Kastigar, supra,* at 460.

Given the proscription against direct or indirect use by the prosecution of immunized testimony, and the publicity that would be attendant to immunized testimony provided at nationally televised congressional hearings, I concluded that a grant of immunity from the Congressional Select Committee, would make it virtually impossible for the Office of Independent Counsel (OIC) to prove an independent source and would effectively shield Mr. Hakim from prosecution. The key would be not only to obtain a congressional grant of immunity, but to ensure that any congressional testimony was obtained in a manner that would maximize its public exposure as well as its likelihood of derivative use (and increase the taint of other witnesses and evidence) and thus frustrate any effort by the OIC to prove an independent source.

Shortly after the investigation began, an attorney at the OIC telephoned me to inform me that it would be serving a subpoena on Mr. Hakim to obtain his passport for examination, and wanted to confirm his home address in California. I responded that it would not be necessary to send an agent to serve a subpoena, as I would accept service on Mr. Hakim's behalf. However, the OIC attorney abruptly cut me off and rather officiously stated that his office was insisting on serving the subpoena on Mr. Hakim *in person*. A few days later the subpoena was served, and after a few weeks, Mr. Hakim's passport, which had been photographed, was returned to him.

As the congressional and OIC investigations geared up, I undertook efforts to persuade both the OIC and the Congressional Select Committee that they should provide immunity to Mr. Hakim in order to gain his cooperation. The attorneys for the Select Committee seemed favorably disposed to my arguments that Congress's oversight responsibility to ascertain the activities of government officials was more important than preserving the possibility of a prosecution, particularly a prosecution of a private citizen who had been enlisted to assist the government in a secret mission.

As my efforts to obtain immunity for Mr. Hakim were ongoing, Mr. Hakim, an international businessman, made plans to go on a lengthy business trip overseas. Before doing so, however, he spoke to an FBI Agent near his home in San Jose (whom he had known for some time) and asked him if there was any reason, in light of the pending investigation, that he could not travel abroad. After checking with officials in Washington, D.C. (presumably the OIC), he told Mr. Hakim that there was no impediment to his plans for foreign travel. Mr. Hakim then left for a business trip to Europe.

While Mr. Hakim was abroad, I received another call from the same OIC attorney who had previously insisted on serving Mr. Hakim personally with a subpoena for his passport. This time, however, he informed me that he had a subpoena for Swiss records, and wanted to know if I would accept service of the subpoena on Mr. Hakim's behalf, since Mr. Hakim was out of the country. I told the attorney that they had insisted on personal service in the first instance, so I would insist on personal service in this instance. I then spoke on the telephone with Mr. Hakim to report on this conversation. I told Mr. Hakim that I could not advise him to stay abroad in order to avoid service of the subpoena, but I did inform him that he had no obligation to reorder his plans for the convenience of the OIC. Mr. Hakim decided to continue his business trip.

While Mr. Hakim was abroad, I was making progress with the Congressional Select Committee. Both the counsel for the House and the counsel for the Senate had a somewhat testy relationship with the OIC. They both felt that the importance of obtaining Mr. Hakim's cooperation (including their assumption that he could produce Swiss corporate and bank records, which were otherwise protected by Swiss bank secrecy laws, and which would likely take the government years to obtain pursuant to a request under the U.S. and Swiss Treaty on Mutual Assistance in Criminal Matters) outweighed the importance of preserving a criminal prosecution, particularly a prosecution of a private individual, and they had encouraged the OIC to afford Mr. Hakim a grant of immunity. When the OIC resisted, the Select Committee decided to go forward on its own, and they informed me that they would be prepared to provide immunity under 18 USC Section 6005. Furthermore, well aware that the OIC wanted to serve a subpoena on Mr. Hakim when he returned to the United States, they agreed that the House and Senate Select Committee would conduct a special session in Paris, France to grant immunity and to take Mr. Hakim's testimony and the production of records.

Consequently, a special session of the House and Senate Select Committee (with some members of Congress in attendance) was convened in Paris. The House counsel, who was taking the lead, accepted my suggestions on how to conduct the testimony in a manner that maximized the protections afforded under the immunity statute against direct or indirect use of Mr. Hakim's testimony. In fact, he followed a written script that I prepared for him. He began by asking general questions and then asked Mr. Hakim if he had personal knowledge of the events regarding the purchase of weapons for the Contras in Nicaragua and the negotiations with Iranian officials regarding the release of American hostages. Then he asked if Mr. Hakim knew whether there were any records relating to those matters; whether he knew where those records were located; whether he had access to those records; and whether he would be able to produce those records. Consequently, when Mr. Hakim produced the records, the records themselves were derivative use of his immunized testimony.

I remember that my law partner and I were quite pleased with the manner in which the proceedings were conducted, and we went out to have a celebratory dinner in Paris. Later that evening, however, we were hit with a dose of cold water when I received a telephone call from Mr. Hakim. During the evening, he had been startled by a knock on his hotel door and an announcement that a representative from the U.S. State Department was there to serve a subpoena. Mr. Hakim refused to open the door or to accept the document, so the State Department representative slid the document under the door.

When my partner and I arrived at Mr. Hakim's hotel room, we reviewed the document that had been left by the State Department representative. The document was not actually a subpoena, but a telex transmission of the contents of a grand jury subpoena for records that had been issued at the behest of the OIC. The return date on the subpoena was only a few days away. I called the prosecutor whose name appeared on the document and told him that I did not believe that slipping a telex transmission under a hotel room door, of the contents of an actual subpoena, was valid service. I asked him to postpone the return date on the subpoena for a week to accommodate the fact that I was out of the country. Although courteous, he refused to do so, and I made arrangements to return to Washington to appear before Chief Judge Aubrey Robinson of the U.S. District Court in a move to quash the subpoena.

By the time I had returned to Washington, Mr. Hakim's

immunized testimony and production of records had been widely reported as front-page news in the national media. The taint clock was ticking. At the hearing before Chief Judge Robinson, the OIC's attorney argued that a subpoena had been validly served, Mr. Hakim should be compelled to produce the requested records, *and that he could not very well deny that he had such records because he had produced them for Congress*. In response, I noted that slipping a telex transmission of the contents of an actual subpoena under a hotel door was not actual service of a subpoena. Furthermore, I noted that the OIC attorney's citation to the reports of Mr. Hakim's immunized testimony was itself derivative use of that testimony in violation of the immunity statute. Finally, I pointed to a somewhat obscure, but nonetheless pertinent, opinion by a well-regarded judge of the U.S. District Court for the District of Columbia, that held that a witness is immune from service of a subpoena while in attendance at or on the way to or from a Congressional hearing. *Youpe v. Strasser*, 113 F. Supp. 289 (1953).

Chief Judge Robinson ruled in my favor from the bench. He advised the OIC's attorney that he would have to try again. (Somewhat inexplicably, the OIC had not, theretofore, availed itself of 18 USC Section 1783, which provides a mechanism to obtain a court order to serve a subpoena on a U.S. national or resident who is in a foreign country.) Once the issue had been properly joined, a grand subpoena was validly served and a date was set for Mr. Hakim to appear before the grand jury.

We then moved to quash the subpoena on Fifth Amendment grounds. The Supreme Court had held in *Fisher v. United States*, 425 U.S. 391 (1976) and *United States v. Doe,* 465 U.S.

605 (1984) that a witness may properly invoke his Fifth Amendment privilege and refuse to produce subpoenaed documents if he can show that the act of production of the documents would be testimonial and might tend to incriminate him by providing evidence of his alleged representative capacity, by confirming the existence and authenticity of the requested documents, and by confirming his possession or control of the documents.

The hearing on the motion to quash was memorable. This time, the OIC was represented by one of its senior attorneys who was an appellate expert; he was also a long-time friend of mine—and a former law clerk for Judge Robinson. (He is now himself a U.S. District Court judge—and one for whom I wrote a letter of recommendation.) The OIC's attorney argued vehemently that the Fifth Amendment did not apply to Mr. Hakim's production of documents and that every person owes a duty to give evidence when properly summoned. He also heavily criticized the protections of Swiss bank secrecy laws, which he lambasted as a shield for criminal activity. When I responded to the OIC's arguments, I relied on *Fisher* and *Doe,* and made the obvious point that under the Fifth Amendment, no person owes a duty to give evidence that might incriminate him. Finally, I addressed the OIC attacks on Swiss bank secrecy. Apparently, my good friend had forgotten that about a year earlier, he had sent me a long law review article he had written on the importance and legitimacy of Swiss bank secrecy laws, which had originally been enacted primarily to protect the identity of European Jews who were shielding their money from the Nazis. I quoted passage after passage from this law review article, which I touted to Judge Robinson as perhaps the seminal article on the importance of Swiss bank secrecy laws.

Chief Judge Robinson was more than a bit amused by my citations to his former law clerk's law review article—he could barely contain his laughter. But he nonetheless denied our motion to quash this subpoena. So on the date set for Mr. Hakim's grand jury appearance we appeared again in Judge Robinson's courtroom. I informed Judge Robinson that Mr. Hakim respectfully declined to comply with the subpoena or Judge Robinson's order mandating compliance. I noted that the only way that we could test the validity of Judge Robinson's ruling was to decline to comply and to have an order of contempt entered by the Court, which we could then appeal to the United States Court of Appeals for the District of Columbia Circuit. I told the Court that I hoped he understood that we meant no disrespect to the Court, but that this was the only way we could litigate the legal issues involved. Judge Robinson said that he completely understood, and when the OIC's attorney asked for $100,000 bond, he summarily dismissed that request and told me that he would await a decision by the Court of Appeals.

We did indeed take the case to the Court of Appeals, where I was once again arguing against my long-time friend on the OIC staff. (Although, as a grand jury matter, the case was filed and was to be argued under seal, on the day of the argument virtually the entire Washington press corps was sitting in the courtroom.) During the argument before the three-judge panel, as the appellant, I went first. The argument went well and at the end of my argument I reserved five minutes of my allotted time for rebuttal. Things did not go well for the OIC—its counsel was questioned rather harshly by the judges. When I arose for my rebuttal, I informed the judges that while I had reserved five minutes I did not see a need to use them, unless the Court had questions. One of the judges on the panel jokingly remarked: "So you don't want to snatch defeat from the jaws of victory."

It was no surprise when the Court's decision was released and Judge Robinson was reversed 3–0. *In re Sealed Case*, 832 F.2d 1268 (D.C. Cir. 1987). I remember thinking at the time how magnificent it was to live in a country where one branch of the government would come to the defense of a mere citizen when another branch of the government was overreaching. To this day, I am still grateful to live in such a country.

Shortly after the Court of Appeals reversed Chief Judge Robinson's decision, I saw him across the room at a reception for the investiture of a new District Court Judge. I was apprehensive as he made a beeline toward me. But when he reached me, he threw his arms around me and congratulated me on my victory in the Court of Appeals. I still marvel at his incredible magnanimity.

In June, 1987, Mr. Hakim appeared before the Iran-Contra Select Committee and a national television audience for three days of public testimony under a grant of immunity. We were confident that his widely viewed and reported public testimony would create such enormous taint that a prosecution by the OIC would be impossible under *Kastigar*. (John Poindexter and Oliver North also testified publicly pursuant to congressional grants of immunity.) Nevertheless, the OIC obtained a sixteen-count felony indictment against John Poindexter, Oliver North, Richard Secord, and Albert Hakim.

My team and our co-counsel were able to assemble overwhelming proof that the prosecution was impermissibly relying on the testimony of tainted witnesses and making derivative use of immunized testimony. For instance, I dealt with the General Counsel at the State Department, who (by the way) was no fan of the OIC. We were able to confirm that all of the State Department officials who testified before the OIC's grand jury, and who would be called as witnesses at trial, had been provided before their grand jury testimony, daily summaries of the immunized testimony before Congress of Messrs. Poindexter, North, and Hakim. Many had actually watched the testimony. We had similar evidence to present regarding other government agencies and officials who were called to testify before the grand jury. Thus, we were quite confident that, if *Kastigar* meant what it said, there was no way that the OIC could establish an independent source free from taint for its evidence.

The case was assigned to Judge Gerhard Gesell, a no-nonsense judge who was brilliant in his heyday. Unfortunately—and I mean no disrespect to Judge Gesell, whom I always admired—he was at the end of his career on the bench, and we were concerned that he was palpably exhibiting signs of his age. Moreover, it was evident that he viewed this nationally followed case as the crowning jewel of his long and distinguished career, and he was intent on having a trial to conduct. Consequently, in probably the most significant case under the immunity statutes in U.S. history, he declined to hold *any Kastigar* hearing, much less a document-by-document, witness-by-witness hearing, as mandated by the Supreme Court, and he set the case for trial. (Ultimately, the United States Court of Appeals ruled in an appeal by Oliver North that *Kastigar* meant what it says. A document-by-document and witness-by-witness hearing should have been conducted by Judge Gesell, at which the OIC would have to meet a very heavy burden of establishing an untainted and independent source for every bit of its evidence. *United States v. North*, 910 F.2d 843 [D.C. Cir. 1990]. The cases of North and Poindexter, who had been convicted at separate trials, were reversed and remanded for the trial court to conduct a thorough *Kastigar* hearing. Judge Gesell made it clear that there was no way he intended to conduct such a hearing as the burden would be impossible to meet, and the OIC dismissed the cases against Poindexter and North.)

As for Mr. Hakim, we successfully moved to sever his case from the cases of Poindexter, North, and Secord; Judge Gesell then set each case for a separate trial. After extended discussions, the OIC agreed to dismiss the sixteen-count felony indictment against Mr. Hakim in return for his agreement to enter a guilty plea to a six-month misdemeanor: aiding and abetting the supplementation of the salary of an officer of the United States in that Mr. Hakim complied with the directions of General Richard Secord to make a payment from the funds in Switzerland of $14,000 to pay for construction of a security fence around Oliver North's home in order to protect his family from a threat that had actually been made by a known international terrorist. That was literally the statement of the offense to which Mr. Hakim would be pleading guilty. I knew that this was truly a nonsensical disposition for a sixteen-count felony indictment and that, if the OIC had exercised any common sense, it would have been wiser for it simply to dismiss the case entirely.

The original plea agreement was also conditioned on the outcome of Mr. North's pending appeal on *Kastigar* grounds of his conviction at trial. If North's appeal was successful and the charges were dropped, then Hakim's plea would be set aside and the case dismissed. Independent counsel Lawrence Walsh and I met personally in chambers with Judge Gesell to explain the conditional plea agreement. He agreed that he would accept such a plea. However, when we subsequently appeared before the judge to enter the plea, Judge Gesell literally did not remember that he had agreed to the conditional plea agreement. He became exercised that we proposed such a plea and he gave Mr. Hakim the choice of pleading to the misdemeanor charge without conditions, or setting the matter down for trial on all sixteen felony counts. Given the risks and expense involved in going to trial, and the unlikelihood that Mr. Hakim would face incarceration on the misdemeanor charge, we reluctantly agreed to forego the conditional plea that had been agreed to.

At Mr. Hakim's subsequent sentencing proceeding, the OIC was embarrassed publicly when Judge Gesell made it clear that he thought the offense to which Mr. Hakim was pleading was nonsensical. He expressed his regret to Mr. Hakim for what he had been put through, commended him for being the person who had successfully negotiated the release by Iranian authorities of hostage David Jacobsen, and sentenced Mr. Hakim to a short period of probation, and a $5,000 fine. Mr. Hakim had Judge Gesell's remarks reprinted and included them in subsequent business presentations.

12

Life with Justice Stevens

by Carol F. Lee

Carol Lee attended Yale, Oxford, and Yale Law School, with a legendary academic record. She first clerked for Judge J. Skelly Wright and went on to serve as a law clerk to Justice John Paul Stevens, about whom she writes. Carol joined Wilmer Cutler & Pickering, became a partner and had a wide-ranging practice. She left Wilmer to become the General Counsel of the Export-Import Bank. Following that job, she became Vice President and General Counsel of the International Finance Corporation, which is an arm of the World Bank Group. Carol is now Special Counsel at Taconic Capital Advisors in New York. She is also a member of the Council of the American Law Institute.

INTRODUCTION

I had the privilege of clerking for Associate Justice John Paul Stevens in the 1982 term of the Supreme Court. My co-clerk Jeff Lehman and I felt that clerking for "our" Justice was the best clerkship in the building. We and the clerks for the other Justices greatly admired Justice Stevens for his intellect and his lawyerly, intellectually honest approach to the law. Jeff and I also appreciated working for a thoughtful and considerate person.

At the time, Justice Stevens was relatively new to the court. In December 1975, he had taken the seat previously occupied by Justice William O. Douglas, so it was only his eighth term as a Justice. (He continued to sit on the Court until he retired in 2010.) In the early 1980s, Justice Stevens was seen as an idiosyncratic moderate who decided cases one by one. His views on the major areas of law were evolving, so clerking for him was an intellectual adventure.

As the second most junior Justice (only Justice Sandra Day O'Connor had joined the Court more recently), Justice Stevens was rarely assigned to write important opinions by the Chief Justice, if the Chief Justice was in the majority and, if not, by the senior Justice in the majority. He did, however, write more concurrences and dissents than any of the other Justices, term after term.

Justice Stevens was the only member of the court who wrote first drafts of opinions himself before giving them to his law clerks for comments and suggestions. Writing helped him crystallize his thinking. He enjoyed discussions and debates with his law clerks.

During the 1982 term and several years before and afterwards, the Justice hired only two law clerks at a time because he didn't need more, even though each Justice was entitled to hire four law clerks. He had a powerful mind and an exceptional memory, so he didn't need his clerks to write bench memos that summarized and analyzed the parties' written briefs.

He also saved his clerks' time on the thousands of petitions for certiorari, i.e., written filings that request the Court to exercise its discretion to hear and decide the petitioners' cases. Justice Stevens required his clerks only to write memos about petitions that we thought were worthy of serious consideration or that another justice had placed on the list for discussion by other members of the Court.

Also, with only two clerks, our chambers could function more informally. Jeff and I had desks in an office just steps away from the Justice's desk. Without scheduling a meeting, the Justice simply came into our office, sat down in the sagging black leather arm chair, and started to talk.

The writings by Justice Stevens that I remember most fondly from the 1982 term are two concurrences and a "statement respecting the denial of certiorari." Each was written in Justice Stevens's distinctive voice. None of them represented or attracted the views of a majority of the nine Justices. In the two cases in which he wrote concurrences, he was the fifth and deciding vote in a 5–4 decision. Both concurrences dealt with fundamental constitutional issues relating to the allocation of power between the federal government and the states, and between the courts and the legislatures. All of them address issues that remain important today—forty years later.

FEDERALISM

One of the basic issues the Court had addressed repeatedly in preceding decades was where the Constitution drew the line between the powers of the federal government under the Commerce Clause (giving Congress power "to regulate Commerce

. . . among the several States . . .") and the matters reserved to the states under the Tenth Amendment ("The powers not delegated to the United States by the Constitution, nor prohibited by it to the States, are reserved to the States respectively, or to the people").

Six years before the 1982 term, the Supreme Court had issued a ruling that the Tenth Amendment curtailed federal power under the Commerce Clause of the Constitution, whose scope the Court had previously given extensive breadth, to regulate state activities that traditionally were performed by state governments (the case was called *National League of Cities v. Usery*). The Court ruled that federal wages and hours legislation could not extend to state public transit employees, because Congress could not "directly displace the States' freedom to structure integral operations in areas of traditional governmental functions."

In the 1982 term, the Court decided a case that involved the application of the federal statute prohibiting age discrimination to a state's mandatory retirement age for fish and game wardens (the case was called *EEOC v. Wyoming*). Justice Brennan won five votes for a narrowly-drawn opinion that upheld the federal age discrimination statute.

Although Justice Stevens joined the majority, his concurring opinion took a stronger position than the majority opinion on the federalism issue. He declared that the ruling six years earlier in the *National League of Cities* case that curtailed the federal power to regulate commerce was so plainly incorrect that, despite the doctrine that the court should adhere to its prior decisions, "the law would be well served by a prompt rejection of [its] modern embodiment of the spirit of the Articles of Confederation" which, of course, the Constitution had replaced. He explained his position in sweeping historical terms: the Commerce Clause "was the Framers' response to the central problem that gave rise to the Constitution itself." Over the course of history, the Court had occasionally given a "miserly construction" to the Commerce Clause, but it had later repudiated those cases to allow federal regulation of an integrated national economy. Justice Stevens's concurring opinion added that he believed that the benefits of a mandatory retirement age exceeded the burdens, but that this personal view was totally irrelevant to his judicial task. This combination of boldness and humility was quintessential Justice Stevens.

Two years after Justice Stevens's concurring opinion, the Supreme Court did what Justice Stevens prescribed by overruling the *National League of Cities* decision (in a case called *Garcia v. San Antonio Metropolitan Transit Authority*). But the pendulum has since swung back in favor of the states. The Court subsequently held that the Tenth Amendment prohibits the federal government from "commandeering" state officials to implement federal mandates (in a case called *New York v. United States*).

The question of where to draw the line between federal and state power continues to be actively litigated today. Once the recourse of states-rights conservatives against a progressive federal regulatory regime, the doctrine has been used most recently by states and cities to resist a variety of federal policies, conservative as well as progressive (for example, sanctuary cities resisting federal enforcement of immigration policies, and California's adoption of stricter auto emission standards than the EPA).

POLITICAL GERRYMANDERING

Another memorable concurrence by Justice Stevens in the 1982 term involved the still vexing issue of political gerry-mandering. A case called *Karcher v. Daggett* was a challenge to a bizarrely-shaped congressional district map created by the New Jersey legislature on a straight party-line vote. One of the New Jersey districts drawn on this map included parts of seven counties and was shaped like a swan with appendages stretching into distant parts of the state. Another district along the coast was "contiguous only for yachtsmen."

In his concurring opinion, Justice Stevens declared that egregious political gerrymandering was unconstitutional because the Equal Protection Clause of the Constitution ("nor shall any State . . . deny to any Person within its jurisdiction the equal protection of the laws") prohibited discrimination against political groups, including citizens whose vote was diluted and therefore unequal as a result of partisan gerrymanders. This was an example of his unconventional views on the meaning of "equal protection."

To show how far the districts in New Jersey departed from the standards of compactness and contiguity, Justice Stevens decided that a color map should be included in the U.S. Reports (the volumes in which Court decisions are officially published). Chief Justice Warren Burger objected that it would be too expensive. As Justice Stevens told the story in his book, *The Making of a Justice: Reflections on My First 94 Years*, he responded that the extra printing cost was less than the amount that he saved the Court by having only two law clerks. In the end, the map was included.

Federal law on political gerrymandering has not developed as Justice Stevens hoped. During his time as a Justice, he tried in vain to persuade the Court to hold that political gerrymandering violated the Equal Protection Clause.

The question remained unresolved for years until 2019, when the Court ruled by a 5–4 vote in a case called *Rucho v. Common Cause* that partisan gerrymandering presented so-called "political questions" that are for the legislatures and not the courts to decide. Chief Justice Roberts justified this conclusion on the ground that none of the proposed tests for identifying impermissible political gerrymanders was judicially discernible and manageable. However, the Chief Justice added that state courts remained free to determine whether redistricting schemes violate state constitutions.

Both before and after the 2019 *Rucho* decision, some state courts, e.g., Alaska, New York, Ohio, Pennsylvania, have invalidated extreme partisan gerrymanders on state law grounds. Justice Stevens would have been heartened by these state court decisions; he was very much in favor of state courts applying their own state constitutions to provide greater rights to citizens than federal law. In 2022, in its decision invalidating a partisan gerrymander, the North Carolina Supreme Court quoted one of Justice Stevens's concurrences about the anti-democratic consequences of gerrymandering. Subsequently, the North Carolina Supreme Court, with a changed membership, vacated the decision and held that challenges to gerrymandering are not justiciable.

At the end of the 2023 term, the Supreme Court in *Moore v. Harper*, rejected the North Carolina legislators' "independent state legislature" theory, preserving the power of state courts to review legislative redistricting decisions on state law grounds.

JURY SERVICE

Finally, a statement by Justice Stevens in the 1982 term changed the course of the law regarding peremptory challenges, which allow lawyers during jury selection to exclude up to a specified number of potential jurors from sitting on the jury without giving any reason. This power had been widely abused to exclude Blacks and others from jury service. In 1965 in a case called *Swain v. Alabama*, the Court had placed an almost insurmountable burden of proof on defendants seeking a remedy for racially motivated peremptory challenges.

An attempt to overturn this 1965 decision came before the Supreme Court in the spring of 1983. In this case, called *McCray v. New York*, the prosecution had exercised peremptory challenges to remove all Blacks from juries that convicted Black defendants. A majority of the Court's members decided not to consider the *McCray* case, a decision called a denial of certiorari. Justices Thurgood Marshall and William Brennan dissented from the denial of certiorari, declaring that the Court should agree to hear the *McCray* case and use it as a vehicle to overturn the *Swain* decision.

In response, Justice Stevens wrote an "opinion respecting the denial of certiorari," in which he acknowledged the importance of the underlying issue but stated that "further consideration of the substantive and procedural ramifications of the problem by other courts will enable us to deal with the issue more wisely at a later date." Justices Harry Blackmun and Lewis Powell joined his opinion. As a result, five Justices were on record as questioning whether the ruling in *Swain* should be overruled.

In the next few years, parties and lower courts took up the Justice's invitation to develop the issues more fully. In 1986, in a case called *Batson v. Kentucky*, the Court overruled *Swain* by a 7–2 vote, establishing procedures for challenging race-based peremptory challenges by prosecutors.

Since then, constitutional limitations have been extended to peremptory challenges by defense counsel and to counsel in civil cases and to peremptory challenges based on gender and ethnicity. One state court recently prohibited peremptory challenges based on sexual orientation. The continued availability of peremptory challenges remains controversial, because the procedures set forth in *Batson* still leave room for abuse. Effective at the beginning of 2022, the Supreme Court of Arizona adopted a rule prohibiting all peremptory challenges in both criminal and civil cases. Potential jurors can still be challenged in Arizona, but only by showing cause.

CONCLUSION

In these three notable judicial writings during the term when I clerked for him, Justice Stevens showed different facets of his jurisprudence. *EEOC v. Wyoming* gave him the chance to articulate his historically-informed view of the purpose of the Commerce Clause and his willingness to overrule precedent, as well as his subordination of his personal policy preferences to his understanding of the law. *Karcher v. Daggett* highlighted his understanding of the ill effects of partisan gerrymandering, a perspective that is now widely recognized, although whether there can be a judicial remedy remains unresolved. And *McCray v. New York* reflected his willingness to let an issue percolate in the lower courts, hoping for the development of practical solutions to a vexing problem of judicial administration. In the 1982 term, Justice Stevens, without a chance to write significant majority opinions, used the opportunities available to him to leave his mark on jurisprudence.[1]

---

1. The author discussed her experience clerking for Justice Stevens and two of the cases discussed in this chapter in "Justice Stevens: An Independent Voice," in New York University School of Law 1992/1993 Annual Survey of American Law, pp. xlvii-li, but the NYU piece was not used as the basis for this chapter. This essay is a substantially revised, expanded, and updated version of Carol Lee's "Three Memorable Opinions," *Judicature,* July-August 2010, pp. 9-10. I appreciate the helpful comments by David J. Seipp, Jeffrey S. Lehman, Nancy S. Marder, and Roger M. Witten.

13

A Pair of Giants

by Louis Cohen

Louis R. Cohen attended Harvard College, Oxford University, and Harvard Law School. He clerked for Justice John Marshall Harlan. He joined Wilmer, Cutler & Pickering (now WilmerHale) in Washington, D.C. where he worked closely with Lloyd Cutler on many matters, including the one he describes here. In 1986, he left the law firm to become Deputy Solicitor General of the U.S. He returned to the firm in 1988 and was a leader of its appellate practice. We worked together on a variety of matters, including the defense of campaign finance reform legislation and the Berlin Accords (an agreement between the U.S. and Germany that provided compensation for forced and slave labor during the Nazi era).

This is the story of how two giants of the Washington, D.C. bar, starting from opposite sides, sold their respective clients on an imaginative solution to a major national problem, and then sold their solution to the Supreme Court.

The giants were Charles Horsky and Lloyd Cutler, and an old cliché is true of them both: we will never see their like again, because in an age of specialization no one will ever match their range, and in a more selfish time no (or few) private lawyers, working for pay, will be so dedicated, for decades, to getting the right outcomes for their country as well as their clients.

Horsky was a partner at Covington & Burling for more than forty years. He founded the Washington, D.C. branch of the American Civil Liberties Union and argued—nobly but unsuccessfully—for Fred Korematsu in the Supreme Court case that upheld the World War II internment of Japanese citizens in the U.S. He was on Robert Jackson's prosecution team at Nuremberg. He persuaded the Supreme Court in *Griffin v. Illinois* that an indigent criminal appellant had a constitutional right to a free trial transcript. He advised two presidents, Kennedy and Johnson, on national capital affairs and was an architect of home rule for DC. He served as Chairman of the National Bankruptcy Conference, Chair of the DC Board of Education, and President of the DC International Horse Show.

Cutler founded Wilmer Cutler & Pickering (now Wilmer-Hale) and, incidentally, served as White House Counsel to two presidents, Carter and Clinton. His other clients included manufacturers with household names, newspapers and television networks, the people of Czechoslovakia, the victims of South African apartheid, Greenpeace, the NAACP, the Metropolitan Opera, and the Rolling Stones. He made major contributions to the law of elections, railroads, securities fraud, the First Amendment, fisheries, strategic arms, auto safety, housing supplies, urban violence, hostage taking, and American intelligence capabilities. And he knew everyone: once, walking past his office, I heard him call out to his secretary "Give Madame Chiang Kai-shek Mr. [Oscar] de la Renta's telephone number."

The major national problem was that beginning in 1970, the Penn Central Railroad and seven other insolvent railroads in the northeast went into reorganization under Section 77, the special railroad provision of the Bankruptcy Act. None of the eight seemed capable of a traditional reorganization—that would require finding a way to operate profitably, and in the 1970s Penn Central alone was losing a million dollars a day, which then was real money. The secured creditors (bondholders) wanted to shut the railroads down, stanch the losses, and foreclose on the railroad properties securing their bonds; their claims did have value (even scrap iron and a long, very skinny piece of real estate have value in liquidation, and the bondholders also foresaw profitable operations in some locations), but shutting down would have crippled the American economy.

Congress's solution, embedded in the Regional Rail Reorganization Act of 1973 (Rail Act), was too clever by half. It created a new government corporation, United States Railway Association (USRA), and instructed it to pick the good parts of the eight railroads and paste them together in a new private "consolidated rail corporation" (Conrail). The railroads were required to keep running, at enormous losses, for the two-plus years Congress expected this process to take. Congress not only assumed that Conrail would be profitable (surely within the money-losing fat railroad system there must be a profitable skinny railroad yearning to get out) but also assumed, even more heroically, that the value of Conrail stock (plus a small amount of cash from the government) would be sufficient to compensate the bondholders.

The Penn Central bondholders immediately challenged the Rail Act's constitutionality, arguing to a three-judge district court that the Rail Act took their property without the just compensation required by the "Takings" clause of the Fifth Amendment by forcing years of loss operations while Conrail was being designed and brought to life, and by forcing them to accept Conrail stock in exchange for their secured claims.

Enter Horsky, who had been Penn Central's lead outside counsel since its creation, and Cutler, who became the newly created USRA's lead counsel soon after the Rail Act was enacted. They were, in substance, on opposite sides, Penn Central wanting as much as possible for its creditors, and USRA wanting to create Conrail at minimal cost to the federal government. But they had known and respected each other for a long time, and in a few phone calls, they came up with a solution: tell the three-judge court that it should allow the Rail Act process to proceed and, if, in the end, the bondholders believed they had not received enough value for their claims, they could sue the United States for just compensation in the Court of Claims under the Tucker Act (which gave that Court jurisdiction over claims against the United States).

The plan didn't please either side. The bondholders wanted cash for their taken property, not Conrail stock, plus the right to bring another lawsuit, years later, for a cash award they would have to prove their right to. They also pointed out that their claims were in the billions of dollars, far larger than any judgment the Court of Claims had ever awarded, and argued that the Court lacked institutional competence to judge the value of security interests in a vast money-losing rail system. The United States wanted the Rail Act process to proceed as written, without an open-ended risk of federal liability that Congress had never contemplated.

But for both Horsky and Cutler, the right starting question was not, "What does my client want?" But "What is the present situation and what, realistically, is the best I can do for the client starting from there?" Putting the question that way enabled them to come up with a creative solution that maximized the bondholders' realistic prospect of recovery and minimized the government's likely payout, all while meeting the national need to keep the railroads running. Horsky persuaded Penn Central's management (but not its bondholders) to endorse the plan, and Cutler persuaded the Departments of Transportation and Justice. He was helped by the fact that President Nixon's Secretary of Transportation was William Coleman, another giant of the DC bar who had known Horsky and Cutler for years, who was reluctant, but willing to listen.

Ultimately, the Horsky-Cutler plan was the defense argued against the bondholders in the three-judge court. But that court rejected the defense, holding there was no indication in the Rail Act that Congress intended to provide a Tucker Act remedy in the Court of Claims and thus the Rail Act did potentially amount to an unconstitutional taking of property without just compensation. In a direct appeal to the Supreme Court, both Horsky and Cutler argued, alongside Solicitor General Robert Bork, and they persuaded the Court that the correct question was not whether Congress intended to provide a remedy under the Tucker Act, but whether it intended to repeal a remedy that already existed; the Court held it did not, and over a powerful dissent by Justice William O. Douglas, upheld the Rail Act and allowed the process to continue.

The whole adventure was a huge failure in some respects.

Conrail began life losing sums as vast as its predecessors, requiring massive infusions (styled loans) of federal dollars, and it did not become profitable until years later, when rail transportation of coal and other commodities increased sharply and Congress forgave billions of dollars in loans. All concerned swiftly agreed that the valuation and compensation task was well beyond the capacities of the Court of Claims, and Congress created an entirely new process that involved years of litigation leading ultimately to a settlement in which the Penn Central bondholders received just under $1.5 billion.

The Supreme Court's ruling, adopting the Horsky-Cutler view, also did some collateral damage that only Justice Douglas, in dissent, noticed at the time. It meant that whenever Congress passes a statute believing it involves no taking of property, but a court later sees a taking, the remedy is not to shut the statute down, or even consider whether that is what Congress would have wanted if it had known there would be a bill to pay, but to carry on and let the Court of Claims deal with the unexpected claim, and Congress deal with the unexpected bill.

But the defense that Horsky and Cutler devised and presented to the Supreme Court from opposite sides served its main purposes. It kept the railroads running, not incidentally allowing a lot of railroad workers to remain employed. It allowed creation of a new railroad that carried major portions of the nation's freight commodities and ultimately became profitable (with a lot of government help). And it led to a process in which the bondholders, who did hold valuable claims, got the compensation they litigated for and ultimately settled for. Not a bad bit of work for the two legal giants.

14

Our First Trustbuster—Senator John Sherman and the Origin of Antitrust

by William Kolasky

Bill Kolasky went to Dartmouth College, where we became friends, and to the Harvard Law School. He clerked for Judge Bailey Aldrich on the U.S. Court of Appeals for the First Circuit. After fulfilling his Army duty, he joined WilmerHale in Washington, D.C. where he became a globally recognized authority on antitrust law. In 2001–2002, Bill served as the Deputy Assistant Attorney General in the Justice Department's Antitrust Division with responsibility for international enforcement and policy. Bill is now a partner in the Washington, D.C. office of Hughes Hubbard & Reed LLP where he continues to practice antitrust law.

The Supreme Court in 1972 called the Sherman Act the Magna Carta of our free-enterprise economy, yet very few probably know much about the man whose name our first and most important antitrust law bears: John Sherman. Here is his story, (an adaptation of an article I wrote that first appeared in *Antitrust Magazine* years ago) which I recount here without the footnote citations that would be found in a law review article.

John Sherman first took up the antitrust cause in the summer of 1888. At the age of sixty-five, Sherman was nearing the end of a remarkable forty-year career in Washington. Over this period, Sherman represented Ohio in the House of Representatives for six years from 1855 to 1861, and then in the Senate for another thirty years, from 1861 until 1897, except for four years when he served as Secretary of the Treasury in the administration of Rutherford B. Hayes. After Sherman retired from the Senate, he served for one year as Secretary of State in the administration of William McKinley.

Sherman died in 1900, too soon to see the Sherman Act become an effective weapon against monopolies and cartels during the administrations of Presidents Theodore Roosevelt and William Howard Taft. Perhaps for that reason, Sherman's obituary in *The New York Times* does not even mention the Sherman Act.

Despite his distinguished record of public service, Sherman spent most of his career in the shadow of his older brother, William Tecumseh Sherman, or "Cump," as he was known, who was one of the Union's greatest heroes of the Civil War. His March to the Sea through Georgia had been instrumental in securing the Union's victory. Following the war, he served as Commanding General of the Army for nearly fifteen years.

While John had a cold, austere personality that earned him the nickname the "Ohio Icicle," Tecumseh was a fixture on the banquet circuit where he was widely sought after as an engaging and entertaining raconteur. When Tecumseh retired from the Army in 1844, he was offered the Republican nomination for President, which he rejected, famously replying that "I will not accept if nominated, and will not serve if elected."

JOHN SHERMAN'S PRESIDENTIAL ASPIRATIONS

In contrast to his brother, John Sherman spent most of the decade of the 1880s actively pursuing the presidency. An 1888 article in *The New York Times* accuses Sherman, while serving as Secretary of the Treasury, of misusing the power of his office to secure the Republican nomination in 1880 by freely promising patronage in return for support, especially in the former Confederate states. Sherman went into the 1880 convention believing he had the full support of the Ohio delegation and a realistic prospect of winning the nomination. At the convention, however, several members of the Ohio delegation defected, supporting James G. Blaine of Maine instead. The convention then deadlocked between Blaine and the former president, Ulysses S. Grant, with Sherman a distant third. After fifty-seven ballots, Blaine and Sherman both threw their support to a dark-horse candidate, fellow Ohioan James Garfield, who had put Sherman's name in nomination. Garfield went on to win the election, only to be assassinated less than one year into his term, leaving his vice president, Chester Arthur, to succeed him.

In 1884, Sherman was again mentioned as a likely candidate, but declined to pursue the nomination in part because the Ohio delegation was again divided between him and Blaine. Sherman also sensed that the widespread dissatisfaction with Arthur's performance made it unlikely that any Republican could be elected. Blaine won the nomination but lost the general election to Grover Cleveland, the first Democrat elected since the Civil War, just as Sherman had feared.

Sherman recognized that 1888 was almost certainly his last

opportunity to reach the White House. This time Sherman was careful to ensure that he had the full support of the Ohio delegation, and many leading newspapers believed his nomination was all but certain. But the convention did not go as they expected. Sherman enjoyed a substantial lead in the early ballots, once coming within just sixty-seven votes of the nomination, but was unable to capture a majority through the first three ballots. On the fourth ballot, New York shifted its votes to Benjamin Harrison, a Civil War hero from Indiana. That shift doomed Sherman's bid. Harrison went on to defeat the Democratic incumbent, Grover Cleveland, in what is often said to have been the most corrupt presidential campaign in American history.

SHERMAN'S REASONS FOR PUSHING ANTITRUST LEGISLATION

Sherman was bitterly disappointed at losing the nomination, which he thought had been stolen from him. Sherman accused the leader of the New York delegation, Tammany boss Thomas C. Platt, of having made a "corrupt bargain" to deliver New York's vote to Harrison. He also accused one of his principal rivals, Governor Russell Alger of Michigan, of buying votes, an allegation that had appeared publicly in a number of contemporary newspaper accounts.

Some have suggested that Sherman's sudden interest in antitrust legislation following the 1888 convention might have been payback directed to Alger. In support, they cite Sherman's extended reference in his principal Senate speech supporting his antitrust bill to a Michigan Supreme Court decision, which had found Alger's Diamond Match Company to be an unlawful combination in restraint of trade under Michigan state law. The *New York Times,* reporting his speech, noted sarcastically that "[o]f course it was with reluctance that Mr. Sherman directed the attention of the Senate and the country to Governor Alger's connection with this 'unlawful' combination."

Another explanation for Sherman's sudden interest in anti-trust in the summer of 1888 may have been that he wanted to protect Republican flanks on what he believed would be the central issue in the upcoming election. Sherman was proud of having "participated in a greater or lesser degree in the fram-ing of every tariff law for forty years," and was a strong propo-nent of protective tariffs to promote domestic industry. In his annual message to Congress the previous December, President Cleveland had directly linked protective tariffs to the spread of domestic trusts, which Cleveland charged "strangled competi-tion." Sherman responded in what he described as a "carefully prepared speech" defending strong tariffs. Three months later, in March 1888, in another Senate speech, Sherman challenged a Democratic Senator, James Beck of Kentucky, who likewise sought to link the two issues, to name any trust that had grown out of tariff laws, declaring that he doubted "whether trusts were caused by the tariff."

Given Democratic efforts to link the two issues, Sherman likely wanted to prevent Democrats from riding the swell-ing antipathy towards trusts to victory in November. Both the Republican and Democratic platforms in the 1888 election included antitrust planks. It was natural for Sherman to have wanted to gain control over the issue, both to reduce the pressure to lower tariff barriers and to assure that whatever legislation was passed was not too radical. And, indeed, one historian writes that Republicans traded their support for Sherman's antitrust bill for Democratic support for the McKinley Tariff law. Consistent with this claim, Sherman in his *Recollections* names the Tariff law, not the Sherman Antitrust Act as "[t]he most important measure adopted" by the 51st Congress.

MOVING ANTITRUST LEGISLATION
THROUGH THE SENATE

Immediately after the 1888 Republican Convention, Sherman began to push for antitrust legislation by introducing a resolution in July, proposing to direct the Committee on Finance, of which he was a ranking member, to develop antitrust legislation designed to promote "free and full competition," which he saw as naturally "increasing production [and] lowering . . . prices." Before the Finance Committee could complete its work, Senator John Reagan, a Democrat from Texas, introduced his own antitrust bill in August, which he asked to have referred to the Judiciary Committee. Senator Sherman objected immediately, asserting that the Committee on Finance was "already in charge of that subject." Senator Reagan quickly receded, but Sherman's old foe on tariff policy, Senator Beck, objected that the Committee on Finance "has got its hands very full just now" and urged that the bill go to either the Commerce or the Judiciary Committees. After a brief debate, the president *pro tem* sided with Sherman and ordered the bill referred to the Committee on Finance. Sherman immediately introduced his own bill as a substitute for Reagan's, entitling it "A bill to declare unlawful trusts and combinations in restraint of trade and production."

Congress recessed shortly thereafter, without taking any further action on the proposed legislation. On January 25, 1889, the first day of the next Congress, Sherman reintroduced his bill, with minor amendments, and brought it to the floor of the Senate for consideration. The debate initially focused on what constitutional authority Congress had to regulate these trusts. Sherman's bill sought to draw the authority from the power of Congress to raise revenue. Senator Reagan argued that this was "a great mistake" and that the authority should instead be grounded on Congress's authority to regulate commerce. When debate resumed ten days later, another Southern Democrat, Senator James George of Mississippi, a former Confederate General and Mississippi State Supreme Court Justice, launched a carefully reasoned and devastating critique of the bill. Expressing his full support for legislation to prevent trusts and combinations, Senator George said that he wanted "effective legislation—legislation that will crush out these combinations and trusts." Senator George charged that Sherman's bill would not reach many of the business combinations at which it was supposedly directed but instead would risk outlawing combinations of farmers or laborers who were simply seeking to earn an honest living.

Senator George's attack effectively killed the bill for the remainder of the 50th Congress. But on the first day of the next Congress, Senator Sherman reintroduced his bill, now S.1. On February 27, 1890, the full Senate again took up the bill, and Senator George repeated his critique. A month later, on March 21, Senator Sherman gave his only extended speech in support of his proposed legislation in which he sought to respond to senator

George's critique. In this speech, Sherman continued to invoke Congress's authority to levy taxes to defend the bill's constitutionality, but now also relied on its authority to regulate interstate commerce. In addition, in defending the bill's provisions, he made two key points that have since helped shape both the final legislation and how the courts have interpreted it.

First, Senator Sherman argued that his bill did not announce a new principle of law, but simply applied "old and well recognized principles of the common law," under which the types of agreements prohibited by his bill would have been treated as null and void. The purpose of his bill, therefore, was simply to give the federal courts the authority "to apply the same remedies against combinations which injuriously affect the interests of the United States that have been applied in the several states to protect local interests."

Second, Senator Sherman denied Senator George's charge that the bill would interfere with lawful trade. Sherman insisted that his bill would "not in the least affect combinations in aid of production where there is free and fair competition," but would only "prevent and control combinations made with a view to prevent competition, or for the restraint of trade, or to increase the profits at the cost of the consumer."

SHERMAN LOSES CONTROL OF THE SHERMAN ACT

Beginning on March 25, 1890, the Senate held three consecutive days of floor debate on the bill. Those Senators who spoke almost all voiced their strong support for legislation regulating trusts, but many continued to voice concern as to the bill's constitutionality and enforceability. Senator Sherman's responses have been described as "impatient and confused." He allowed multiple amendments to be added, turning the bill into what some called a "tangled mess."

On March 27, two senior Republican senators—George Edmunds of Vermont and George Hoar of Massachusetts—seeing that things were spinning out of control, essentially took over the debate. While voicing support for the need to regulate trusts more effectively, each questioned both the bill's provisions and the basis for Congress's constitutional authority to act.

Their remarks emboldened a relatively junior Senator, Orville Platt of Connecticut, to deliver a scathing attack on the bill. Platt closed his remarks with a stinging rebuke of the more senior Sherman: I am sorry, Mr. President, that we have not had a bill which had been carefully prepared." Rather, he said, "[t]he conduct of this Senate for the past three days—and I make no personal allusions—has not been in the line of the honest preparation of a bill to prohibit and punish trusts. It has been in the line of getting some bill with that title that we might go to the country with. We should legislate better than that."

Having successfully resisted having his bill referred to the Judiciary Committee on multiple occasions over nearly two years, Sherman now lost control of the Act that would bear his name. Over Sherman's objection, the Senate voted 31–28 to refer the bill to the Judiciary Committee with instructions to report back within twenty days. The Judiciary Committee reported back less than one week later with a new bill. The new bill deleted all of Sherman's language except for the title and replaced it with the language now so familiar to all antitrust lawyers.

In section 1, it declared unlawful "Every contract, combination in the form of trust or otherwise, or conspiracy, in restraint of trade or commerce among the several States, or with foreign nations." And in section 2, it provided that "Every person who shall monopolize, or attempt to monopolize, or combine or conspire with any other person or persons to monopolize any part of the trade or commerce among the several States, or with foreign nations, shall be guilty of a misdemeanor."

This language resolved the questions about Congress's constitutional authority, solidly grounding the legislation in Congress's power to regulate interstate or foreign commerce. The Senate, after a brief debate, quickly passed the Judiciary Committee's substitute bill with only minimal changes. The House subsequently approved a nearly identical bill and, following conference, both houses passed the Sherman Act nearly unanimously.

After the Judiciary Committee reported its substitute bill, Senators Edmunds and Hoar assumed leadership of the debate on the Senate floor, Senator Sherman did not further participate in the debate, apart from this one brief statement: "I wish to state that, after having fairly and fully considered the amendment proposed by the Committee on the Judiciary, I shall vote for it, not as being precisely what I want, but as the best under all the circumstances that the Senate is prepared to give in this direction." Sherman was considerably less circumspect in sharing his true feelings in an interview he gave to the *St. Louis Globe-Democrat* on April 8. The paper reported: "The bill ... will, in the opinion of the Senator, be totally ineffective in dealing with combinations and Trusts. All corporations can ride through it or over it without fear of punishment or detection. . . ."

Senator Hoar later wrote sarcastically in his autobiography that, "In 1890 a bill was passed which was called the Sherman Act, for no other reason that I can think of except that Mr. Sherman had nothing to do with framing it whatever." Hoar, a distant cousin of Sherman's, went on to claim that he, not Sherman, "was the author of the bill." On the floor of the Senate that same year, Hoar added that "the Sherman antitrust law . . . ought to be called the anti-Sherman trust law, because it was passed under his vigorous protest."

Senator Edmunds later disputed Senator Hoar's claim of authorship, although he agreed that Sherman was not the author. Unlike Hoar, Senator Edmunds graciously credited the entire Committee as sharing in the act's authorship: "It would be correct to say that nearly every member of the committee was the author of the bill, for my work in drawing it up was merely putting into logical shape what every member of the committee had participated in."

Nevertheless, in the end, it still seems fair to give John Sherman the credit that history has accorded him by attaching his name to the Sherman Antitrust Act. Sherman, after all, was the initial sponsor of the legislation and moved it through the legislative process for nearly two years, almost to the eve of its enactment. And the substitute law the Judiciary Committee drafted was fully consistent with the purpose of the legislation as Sherman described it in his speeches on the floor of the Senate when it was being debated. Sherman, therefore, fully deserves recognition as our first trustbuster.

15

Stabbing from the Shadows: My Flawed Hero

by Nelson Johnson, JSC (Ret.)

Judge Nelson Johnson practiced law for 31 years (Martindale Hubbell A-V Rating) prior to being appointed to the New Jersey Superior Court. While on the bench, Johnson served in the Civil Division for 13 years, until mandatory retirement in 2018. He presided over 200(+) jury trials and settled hundreds more. During his final five years, he handled Mass Tort Claims, involving product liability claims against pharmaceutical companies. Johnson is "Of Counsel" to the Hankin Sandman Law Firm in Atlantic City where he conducts mediations. He remains a very active non-fiction author and speaks before bar associations, business groups, college students, and library audiences. Johnson is the author of Boardwalk Empire: The Birth, High Times and Corruption of Atlantic City *("B/E" inspired the HBO series of the same name);* The Northside: African Americans and the Creation of Atlantic City; Battleground New Jersey: Vanderbilt, Hague, and Their Fight for Justice; *and* Darrow's Nightmare: The Forgotten Story of America's Most Famous Trial Lawyer. *(Darrow's Nightmare is on a path toward film.)*

I was first drawn to Arthur T. Vanderbilt, the namesake of "Vanderbilt Hall" at NYU Law School, shortly after beginning my law practice. From elementary school forward, law school was always in my sights. While an undergraduate at St. John's, my political philosophy and history professors persuaded me that lawyers had a duty to push the envelope of the law on issues affecting society. The '60s were god-awful. When I began practicing law in 1974, America was still living in the shadow of the assassinations of JFK, MLK, and RFK. How could I not see myself as a progressive attorney?

So it was, with that mindset, I found myself doing research in my law firm's library one Saturday morning. Seated at a long table covered with books I had pulled from the shelves, I stumbled upon *Fox v. Snow (6 NJ 12 [1950])*. Or more precisely, another ruling had steered me to the dissenting opinion of Arthur T. Vanderbilt, New Jersey's first Chief Justice under its 1947 Constitution. The ruling in that case was one in which six of New Jersey's seven Supreme Court justices rejected the petition of a niece seeking release of funds bequeathed to her by her aunt. The funds had transferred automatically to the uncle's account upon the aunt's death and now, both aunt and uncle were dead. Despite the aunt's obvious intent that her niece should receive the disputed funds, the court nullified the aunt's "gift over" to her niece. Vanderbilt was annoyed with his colleagues and launched into a lesson on the growth of the common law.

In his trenchant dissent, Vanderbilt took his brethren to school on the need for courts to be responsive to life's changes. "It is as important to the growth of the law that it should have the inherent power to cast off outmoded or erroneous rules . . . To hold, as the majority opinion implies, that the only way to overcome the unfortunate rule of law that plagues us here is by legislation, is to put the common law in a self-imposed straight jacket . . . The doctrine of *stare decisis* neither renders the courts impotent to correct their past errors nor requires them to adhere blindly to rules that have lost their reason for being . . . The common law would be sapped of its life blood if *stare decisis* were to become a god instead of a guide . . . Every change in the law by judicial decision necessarily creates rights in one party to the litigation and imposes corresponding duties on the other party. This is the process by which the law grows and adjusts itself to the changing needs of the times." With that lone dissent, Arthur T. Vanderbilt (ATV) entered my pantheon of legal heroes. Years later, it was necessary for me to revisit some of my political/historical readings while in college. Eventually, those readings led me back to Vanderbilt.

Not long after New Jersey's voters approved casino gambling in Atlantic City, I was asked to represent that city's planning board. During my several years working in City Hall (early 1980s), I began a quest to make sense of the dysfunction surrounding me. What spurred my efforts toward writing *Boardwalk Empire: The Birth, High Times and Corruption of Atlantic City*, was the career of political boss Enoch "Nucky" Johnson (no relation) whose career ultimately inspired Steve Buscemi's role in the HBO series.

In conducting my research, I returned to a biography of long-time Jersey City Mayor, Frank "I am the Law" Hague. That book, *The Boss: The Hague Machine in Action*, had been assigned reading at St. Johns. I returned to it because I had recalled a portion discussing the relationship between Democratic Mayor

Hague and Republican Nucky Johnson. On my second reading, I picked up on something I hadn't noticed as a college student: *The Boss* contained multiple court citations. I found that unusual. Also, the author, David Dayton McKean, was a speech professor at Dartmouth College. Why had a guy in New Hampshire—with no prior historical writings—written a biography of Jersey City Mayor Frank Hague?

After *Boardwalk Empire*, I wrote its sequel, *The Northside: African Americans and the Creation of Atlantic City*. Then, in need of a diversion other than Atlantic City, I stumbled upon *Order in the Courts: A biography of Arthur T. Vanderbilt*, written by his grandson, Arthur T. Vanderbilt II. This excellent book was what I was looking for to learn more about ATV. I found it alternately satisfying and frustrating. While this biography had a lot of useful and interesting material, I was struck by the absence of a discussion of the bitter rivalry and mutual disdain between ATV and Mayor Frank Hague. I decided to learn more about ATV. Eventually, my curiosity led me back to McKean's book, *The Boss*.

Revisiting McKean's book for a third time, I was interested in Frank Hague the person. That interest led me to the Jersey City Library where a treasure trove of information awaited me. As I learned with Atlantic City, many communities have residents who assume the role of what I refer to as "folk historians." Despite little training in historical research, they love their community and collect information on their town's history. What I found was an eye-opener. Awaiting me in Jersey City was a large number of carefully assembled mini-biographical sketches on various aspects of Frank Hague's career and life. The detractors and supporters were roughly equal, something I hadn't expected.

What became increasingly apparent in my research was that for Hague and his supporters, New Jersey politics was a religious war. That war was fought between the entrenched WASP Republicans of Essex County and elsewhere, led by ATV against the Irish Catholic Democrats of Hudson County along with first-generation Jewish professionals led by Hague. I made several more visits and combed through the stacks of materials before Frank Hague, the person, came into focus.

I then visited the Newark Library. Though helpful, Vanderbilt hadn't played anywhere near as large a role in his city's history as Hague had in Jersey City.

From having read *Order in the Courts*, I knew that one vital source of information on ATV was the Olin Library at Wesleyan University in Middletown, Connecticut. Throughout his career, ATV was a blur of motion, yet somehow he found time to keep a record of his exploits, all securely stored away in the archives at the Olin Library. Very few lawyers today can review the records of ATV's infinitely broad client base, nationwide contacts, or the varied legal and political issues he pursued throughout his career without feeling like small-time players. The archival catalogue alone is imposing, more than 100 boxes. The effort and care that went into maintaining (40+) years of documents told me that Vanderbilt was someone who believed he had earned a place in American history.

Were ATV and Hague alive today, they'd be annoyed to learn that I'd tried my best to treat them in an even-handed manner in my book *Battleground New Jersey: Vanderbilt, Hague and Their Fight for Justice*. In spite of the enormous gap in their education, heritage, and style, Vanderbilt and Hague shared common traits.

Neither had casual moments with anyone but trusted allies; neither had time for opinions that didn't suit their agenda; neither drank alcohol or had dalliances with women. Both exuded an intensity that either attracted people or repelled them; both craved power to bend the world to their vision; both were ruthless—Vanderbilt when he had to be, Hague because he knew no other way.

Yet at the end of the hunt, what I learned was that my hero ATV was even more complicated than I had originally thought. Despite his superior education, prowess as an attorney, and reputation as a legal reformer, in his battle with Frank Hague, Arthur Vanderbilt stooped to a level his supporters and this historian could never have imagined. The contents of Box 96 at Olin Library reveal it all.

Before joining the faculty at Dartmouth College, Professor McKean was on the staff at Princeton University, where he taught speech. During those years, 1932–1938, McKean was active in New Jersey politics; he ran for and won two terms in the state Assembly. While in Trenton, he got to see Frank Hague's handiwork up close and concluded that the biggest hurdle to lifting New Jersey's state government out of its swamp of corruption was Frank Hague. McKean and Vanderbilt both valued the difference between the spoken and the written word. They knew that ink on paper had greater impact, and although there had been many articles critical of Hague in major news publications, none inflicted lasting damage. Both men wanted a book.

Not long after relocating to New Hampshire, McKean got to work on a book about Frank Hague and the Hudson County Democratic machine. History doesn't tell us who reached out for whom, but we do know that sometime in 1939, ATV and McKean began their collaboration on what was to be one of the great biographical hatchet jobs in American history. Delivered in a breezy tone yet presented as a serious study of a big city mayor's life and times, the book and its author(s) had an agenda, namely, the political assassination of their subject. Their alliance began when ATV advanced funds to McKean to carry him over the summer of 1939, enabling him to keep working on their project.

Because Vanderbilt believed that Hague had to be battered, and since that couldn't happen through the election process or the courts, he would do it with the written word. ATV decided that he would stab at Frank Hague from the shadows. The mannerly progressive lawyer who fretted over a court system in which only the well-connected could count on fair play wasn't troubled by his covert undertaking. He was determined to have a full-length book damning Hague, a book scholarly in appearance, yet calculated to destroy any aura of respectability arising from Hague's relationship with President Franklin Roosevelt. Vanderbilt wanted a book that would be read not only in New Jersey but nationally. After all, the Mayor of Jersey City was also vice chairman of the Democratic National Committee, and it was only fitting that his friends nationwide should have a chance to learn more about his career. Thus, the book had to be placed with a major publisher with outlets in all forty-eight states. Though Box 96 doesn't tell us precisely when Arthur and David began their work, we know the first fruits of their labors—a draft manuscript—was delivered for Vanderbilt's review in January 1940. Not long afterward, Vanderbilt found the prestigious Houghton

Mifflin Company of Boston, a publisher that did both popular and scholarly works.

Yet Arthur and David's efforts were only semi-scholarly. Their intent was to destroy Frank Hague's character. Rather than dispassionately portraying the full context of one of the largest figures in New Jersey's history—a figure whose life spoke much about the times he lived in—Arthur and David ruthlessly maligned Mayor Hague. Putting it kindly, Box 96 confirms that the president of the American Bar Association—so committed to truth and justice—was not above cherry-picking the public record in libeling Frank Hague. Vanderbilt personally drafted multiple revisions to McKean's book—far greater than mere editing, akin to being a co-author. The two were very selective in weaving a story that was mostly accurate, yet decidedly misleading, presented as thoughtful history.

McKean's solicitation of Vanderbilt's thoughts, including rewrites, is apparent from their correspondence. One such instance was a chapter on "socialized medicine." Writing to Vanderbilt, McKean stated, "I hope you will feel free, as before, to comment. I also hope you find this amusing."

When one reads the mocking criticism of Hague's feat of extending universal medicine to Jersey City's residents, the co-authors cynicism is palpable. Health care for the poor, particularly pregnant women, was a cornerstone of the progressive movement, yet in *The Boss* the hospital was all about politics. In chapter ten, "Turning Hospital Beds into Votes: Socialized Medicine under the Hague Machine," Vanderbilt and McKean lambaste Hague's life's work:

In his recognition of the political possibilities of hospitalization Hague stands unique among American bosses: he alone has seen the way that lavish medical care can be used to disarm criticism, and that it is practicable to have children literally born into the organization, obligated to it from the first squalling moment. Cared for during recurrent illnesses of youth, they come to associate health itself with the generous political party that has guided their city for decades; they will no more vote against Hague than against life.

In an attempt to minimize Hague's trophy achievement, McKean recounts a sanitized history of Jersey City's public hospital system. He would have the reader believe that the medical center was not the bold and transformative idea that it was, but rather the latest installment of previously planned efforts to provide health care to city residents. The book leaves out an important point: historically, the Irish were severely discriminated against by the WASP-operated health clinics. Completely ignored by Vanderbilt and McKean is the fact that it wasn't until 1921—when Hague was consolidating power in his second term as mayor—that anything in the way of serious health care for the working poor was provided. Jersey City's WASPs totally ignored the health care needs of the immigrant class; it took Hague to deliver medical care to everyone.

Jersey City Medical Center was gigantic, comprising seven towers and several hospitals: the Medical Building, providing what's called "urgent care" today; a Tuberculosis hospital; a Psychiatric hospital; a Hospital for Infectious Diseases; and most prominently, the "Margaret Hague Maternity Hospital," named for Hague's mother. For the Irish of Jersey City, the maternity hospital was a giant step from being born on a kitchen table. In its prime, the hospital was unsurpassed in its low rates of maternal and infant mortality. *The Boss* reduced the hospital to a place where Jersey City's residents were "born into the organization, obligated to it from the first squalling moment." Despite this demeaning take on the hospital, Jersey City's residents knew that if good health abandoned them, they weren't alone; Hague's hospital would care for them.

Another issue that received Vanderbilt's and McKean's deceptive treatment involved a complicated lawsuit, comprised of multiple court rulings, sprawling over many months. *In re Hague* was the litigation discussed in *The Boss* that provoked this historian's curiosity and raised doubts about the book's even-handedness.

Shortly after the 1928 gubernatorial primary, Republican State Senator Clarence Case declared war on Frank Hague. That was the primary in which party-endorsed reform-minded Judge Robert Carey went down to defeat as a result of 20,000(+) Hudson County "Republicans for the day" voted for Morgan Larson (a stone-cold loser) in accordance with a deal struck by Hague with Atlantic City Republican boss Nucky Johnson.

Enraged by Hague's manipulation of the primary, the Republican legislature launched an inquisition into Hague's finances. Hague was summoned to Trenton and ordered to answer questions about his personal assets. He declined to appear;

litigation ensued. These court proceedings are recounted in *The Boss*. Emphasizing the farcical nature of a mayor being able to amass a fortune while receiving a salary of $8,000, Vanderbilt and McKean assailed Hague's ill-gotten wealth. Tracing funds and cash payments, identifying Hague's partners in crime and connecting the dots to show the intersections of politics and money, *The Boss* tells the story more clearly than most chroniclers of the time. Although the details of Hague's corruption are consistent with the Senate Committee's findings, that's only part of the story.

Unraveling Vanderbilt's quilt of partial truths in discussing *In re Hague* requires a broader discussion of those proceedings than Vanderbilt and McKean presented. When the legislature issued a warrant for Hague's arrest, the mayor's lawyers petitioned the Chancery Court where longtime Hudson County politician Vice Chancellor John J. Fallon heard the petition. The Republicans asserted conflict of interest and were outraged by Fallon's willingness to hear the petition. He wasted little time in granting an order, finding no legal justification to arrest Hague. Both Fallon's refusal to recuse himself, and his order voiding the arrest warrant, were challenged by Senator Case and the Republicans in an appeal to the then final appellate court, the Court of Errors and Appeals. As described in *The Boss*:

> The committee was curious about the sources of all this cash money, but Mayor Hague "declined to answer." The committee then brought him before the whole legislature, where he still declined to answer. He said that the questions were personal and beyond the right of legislative inquiry; he was arrested for contempt

[note to reader: he was *not* arrested], but he immediately applied to Vice Chancellor Fallon, former Hudson County assemblyman and county counsel, who granted a writ of habeas corpus on the ground that the legislature was usurping a judicial function in asking questions that were designed to show a criminal conspiracy. The state appealed to the Court of Errors and Appeals, which by dividing evenly six to six, upheld the vice chancellor. Mayor Hague said in a statement: "I am very much pleased and satisfied with the decision. It is exactly what I expected." The decision cut the ground from under the Case Committee; they were never able to explain the mayor's great affluence.

There are problems with this recitation. The full story is a lot more than "six to six." There were five separate court rulings on the issues raised by *In re Hague*. Vanderbilt and McKean cite only one. Adding further to the deception, the court citation used is for a different ruling than the one that yielded the six-to-six vote.

Most importantly, *The Boss* never discusses the fifth and final decision. The authors would have the reader believe that the final vote of the high court was a tie, but the six-to-six vote merely dealt with the preliminary question of the arrest warrant. Not discussed was the fact that following that ruling the litigation continued and a final determination was made on the legislature's authority to compel Hague to answer questions. That decision arrived thirteen months later on May 19, 1930. By a vote of ten to one, the Supreme Court rejected the Republicans' arguments.

What's more, the judge who wrote the opinion chiding the legislature was Chief Justice William Gummere, a lifelong Republican and no friend of Frank Hague. Gummere was the dean of New Jersey's legal community. His role as one of the most enlightened jurists in an antiquated court system made him a highly regarded figure. Yet Gummere wasn't impressed with the Republicans' arguments. He viewed them as cheap political grandstanding; to him, the legislators had behaved no better than the bully they had condemned. Yet somehow, no mention of Gummere's ruling found its way into *The Boss*.

Vanderbilt's spin on the case law coming out of *In re Hague* fell far short of how he would have treated it were he lecturing on the investigatory powers of a state legislature in his class at NYU Law School.

Shining additional light on Vanderbilt's conduct, Box 96 contains a memo from one of his former students, labeled "D.A.C. to A.T.V." The memo is etched in frustration. "D.A.C.," Dominic A. Cavicchia, was a Newark lawyer who had been Vanderbilt's student at NYU. In November of 1940, Professor Vanderbilt gave Cavicchia an assignment he could never have imagined, years earlier. That November, Cavicchia wrote to Vanderbilt reporting on his meeting with Houghton Mifflin's executives in Boston at which he represented Vanderbilt on his desire to step back from *The Boss*. Essentially what Vanderbilt wanted was for the publisher to remove his name entirely from its files. He wanted his prior correspondence vouching for McKean and playing down the potential of a libel lawsuit by Hague returned to him. Finally, Vanderbilt wanted the original invoice for his purchase of 500 books returned and recreated to show Cavicchia as the book buyer. Houghton Mifflin's executives rejected all of Vanderbilt's requests. Trying earnest pleas, veiled threats, and bluster, Cavicchia couldn't gain much traction with the publisher.

Box 96 does not reveal Vanderbilt's thoughts on the events in Boston; there is no reply memo from Vanderbilt. But Vanderbilt understood that he was at a dead end with Houghton Mifflin. He moved on to the next phase—distributing *The Boss* throughout New Jersey and the nation. With the help of Joseph Fuhrman, a close ally and local publicist, Vanderbilt strategized the marketing of McKean's book, creating a mailing list and developing the road map for placing the book in the hands of journalists who would review it favorably.

Vanderbilt did not want to miss out on any of the mischief he was creating, and one of the first things he did before Houghton Mifflin distributed the book was to enter in a contract with Burrelle's Press Clipping Bureau, Inc., of New York City. Burrelle's duties were to "Take all references to the book . . ." We don't know how much time Vanderbilt spent reading the press clippings, but Box 96 contains numerous clippings of reviews and news articles about the book. Some are more sensational than others, but Hague doesn't fare well in any of them.

Vanderbilt's goal was to reach as many national Democratic leaders as possible in order to taint Hague in their eyes. He succeeded. Not long afterward, Frank Hague retired. Unlike many other political bosses, he was never convicted of a crime, and died quietly at home with his family.

As to New Jersey's constitutional reform, Vanderbilt had fought the good fight for decades on end, and finally won. The new court system that emerged under his leadership caught the attention of judges, lawyers, and scholars from across the nation. Vanderbilt's decisions are a model of clarity and precision, and embody progressive thinking on the status of law in America.

Yet one decision still stands apart for this historian. Unimaginably, it was a case in which compliance with judicial ethics would have obligated the chief justice to disqualify himself. That's because Canon 4 of 1950, "A judge's official conduct should be free from impropriety or the appearance of impropriety," clearly barred his involvement. It was a case on which Vanderbilt wrote the opinion for the state Supreme Court on a 4–3 vote. It was an appeal in which Frank Hague was a party.

Despite Hague's complete retirement from politics, the new people in City Hall wanted a pound of flesh, or more precisely, they wanted $15 million (about $300 million today) from him—a nice round number for which there was little factual or legal basis. The complaint filed with the court included a stanza endlessly repeated: "theft, defrauds, and extortions" to describe a portion of Hague's *modus operandi* while serving as mayor. In addition to humiliating Hague, the stated purpose of the lawsuit was to return to the public treasury all of the funds of which the city was purportedly defrauded through the 3 percent payroll kickback scheme, or "rice pudding day." Hague's organization had perfected the scheme to such an extent that most city employees viewed the payments as akin to union dues.

Nonetheless, the new mayor and city commissioners demanded the money be returned. Recognizing political revenge when he saw it, the trial court judge dismissed the city's lawsuit, terming the allegations of the complaint "contradictory, ambiguous, and confusing." In the opinion of the trial court judge,

"The complaint appears to me to be completely stultified by incongruities."

The city appealed to the Appellate Division. Impatient with the normal appeal procedures, Vanderbilt short-circuited the process by granting certification, despite neither party having requested an expedited review. It's inconceivable that anyone else on the court knew of the chief justice's ties to McKean.

Vanderbilt's ruling was shamelessly pontifical. Quoting one of his earlier opinions on political corruption, he wagged his finger at Hague and his codefendants, stating, "As fiduciaries and trustees of the public weal they are under an inescapable obligation to serve the public with the highest fidelity."

Yet, the city's pleadings were fuzzy on whether city government was entitled to the $15 million or if it should be returned to the employees. The fatal inconsistencies of the city's pleading are revealed by language trying to have it both ways: "All such money ["rice pudding"] extorted by defendants from city employees under defendants' 3 percent extortion scheme were and are subject to be forfeited to the city for its own use and benefit, or as trustee for the use and benefit of defrauded employees." The contradiction of the relief sought was obvious. Most of Jersey City's employees were willing participants in the scheme, especially the ones with no-show jobs. So why couldn't the money simply be returned to the city's treasury without equivocation? What was the need for the city to serve as "trustee" for the supposedly defrauded employees who had participated in the scheme? Plaintiffs probably envisioned a shakedown of Hague with the money paid into a trust for city employees aligned with the current administration.

Yet another problem with the city's pleadings, which the trial court noted when dismissing the complaint, was the general allegations of fraud. For centuries, courts have required facts supporting fraud to be stated with a fair amount of detail so a defendant knows exactly with what he has been charged.

Neither the discrepancy in the relief sought nor lack of detail of the fraud claim troubled Vanderbilt. For him, "The substantial question is whether they [Hague and company] can be permitted in law to do this [orchestrate the 3 percent scheme]." Obviously, the law doesn't condone "rice pudding," but as noted by the trial court and the three dissenting justices (one Democrat and two Republicans), that is not the issue. On a motion to dismiss a complaint, the inquiry is whether or not the pleadings state a coherent cause of action for which relief can be granted. Justice Heher pointed out to the chief justice that, in his rush to remand the city's lawsuit back to the trial court, he had overlooked one of his own rulings in which he had opined years earlier, "While a party may claim inconsistent claims or defenses and may be heard to argue inconsistent principles of law, he cannot be heard here to contend for two diametrically opposed set of facts." In taking one last swipe at Frank Hague, Vanderbilt was willing to ignore that it wasn't legally, or factually, sustainable for any money obtained from a judgment against Hague to be payable to both the city and to Hague's coconspirators in the extortion scheme.

Vanderbilt's ruling returned the city's lawsuit to the trial court, but nothing came of it. The history of any further court proceedings is a mystery; no records survive. Hague never paid a single dollar to Jersey City, and he died several months later on New Year's Day, 1956—sixteen days shy of his eightieth birthday.

Thanks to *The Boss*, Hague's name is synonymous with political corruption; in turn, for many people, political corruption is synonymous with New Jersey. Yet other portions of Hague's legacy include tens of thousands of babies born on clean sheets in a first-rate hospital and a generous hand lent to a generation of newcomers. Frank Hague was a complicated and flawed person, yet few people have wielded power as skillfully as he did. Given his start as a sixth-grade dropout, living in the abject poverty of Jersey City's Horseshoe, he has no peer in American history.

Eighteen months following Hague's passing, Vanderbilt died on June 16, 1957, three weeks shy of his sixty-ninth birthday. Though Vanderbilt's uncompromising nature and hatred for Frank Hague reveal an equally complicated and flawed person, that's hardly the measure of the man. More than half a century after his passing, the NYU Law Center that he established has flourished and expanded its mission in ways that do Vanderbilt proud. His legacy from his years on the bench is that the New Jersey Judiciary remains one of the most highly regarded state court systems in America. In terms of decisions followed by other state courts, New Jersey is one of the more influential in the nation. To this day, judges and scholars travel from foreign countries to study how New Jersey's court system operates. If there were a hall of fame for judges, Arthur Vanderbilt would be a member.

16

The Stand-up Guy

by Roger M. Witten

Call the client "Ted." Ted grew up on the wrong side of the tracks and was not a very good citizen until he joined the U.S. Army where he excelled. He won promotions and decorations for his service and bravery in Vietnam. Following Vietnam, he earned a college degree, found his way to responsible positions in respectable companies, and even served in an informal capacity on a Presidential Transition committee.

That is where he met and became buddies with "Joe." Down the road a bit, Joe learned, in connection with his job, certain material non-public information relating to a merger that would soon be announced. Joe "tipped" Ted. Each bought the target company's stock at a low price before the market knew about the planned merger and, after the merger had been publicly announced, each sold at a considerable profit.

Little did they know that the SEC routinely monitored large stock trades immediately before and after such mergers to find any evidence of insider trading. The monitors spotted Joe and Ted's trades, found them suspicious, and began an inquiry.

When it became apparent that prosecutors were initiating a

criminal inquiry, Joe decided to cooperate by voluntarily telling the truth, which implicated Ted. Not surprisingly, Joe did not alert Ted. Meanwhile, Ted considered himself to be a "stand-up guy" who would not "rat" on a friend. So, when the prosecutors questioned him, he falsely stated that he traded the stock based on information he had overheard in a bar. No one would, or did, believe that story.

At this late date, Ted retained us and shortly thereafter he bestowed upon me the nickname "Witless." It was clear to Witless that the "stranger in a bar story" would not fly and that, if Ted did not recant, he would be indicted and convicted based on Joe's confession and other evidence. At length, Ted agreed to recant.

We met with the prosecutors to explore the possibility of a plea agreement that would involve a guilty plea, but not incarceration. We made a proffer of his truthful testimony that effectively acknowledged that his prior statements were untruthful. And we offered Ted's full cooperation going forward. Not surprisingly, the prosecutors viewed our offer as "too little, too late" to warrant leniency.

It was clear that we needed to offer something else to entice the prosecutors to bargain with us. While we were confronting this dilemma, a rabbit emerged from a hat: it turned out that Ted was positioned to disclose a second, entirely unrelated and more serious offense, which was unknown to the prosecutors.

So we met again with the prosecutors. We made a proffer that Ted would disclose this information and voluntarily cooperate in return for leniency in the insider-trading case. This piqued the prosecutors' interest. After a great deal of back and forth, we negotiated some leniency in the insider-trading case in return for his full cooperation. But all this was conditioned on Ted's taking and passing an FBI lie detector test relating to the second matter.

As part of our preparation, we thought it prudent for us to administer our own lie detector test to see how it went. We retained a consultant who had considerable experience with administering and interpreting the results of such tests. The results of these practice sessions did not inspire confidence. Ted, however, appeared unconcerned: "Don't worry, Witless."

The appointed day for the FBI test came. Ted passed. The FBI found no indication that he was lying. We breathed a happy, albeit somewhat puzzled, sigh of relief.

Someone in Ted's delicate position should typically lie low. Not Ted. He invited his friends to a Georgetown bar which he had festooned with a banner that read: "Ted 1–FBI 0." Seriously!

Some time passed as we negotiated the plea agreement and dealt with issues arising from the pre-sentence report. The prosecutors agreed not to advocate for or against incarceration. So the outcome was not free from doubt.

Come the sentencing hearing date. I arrived early to my office. There, sitting in our reception area, was the stand-up guy dressed head-to-toe in an old-fashioned prisoner uniform holding a placard that said "Another satisfied client of" our law firm. We laughed hysterically.

After a wardrobe adjustment, we went to court. The judge sentenced Ted to conditional probation and a fine. Ted would not go to prison.

For many years thereafter, the stand-up guy would call me from time-to-time to check in on Witless. And for many years, he never missed sending something to our daughters on their birthdays.

SECTION III

EXPERIENCES

17

The Case of a Lifetime

by Harriet Newman Cohen

Harriet N. Cohen attended Barnard (B.A. cum laude), Bryn Mawr (M.A.), and, as the mother of four growing daughters, ages 8–18, attended Brooklyn Law School 18 years after getting her M.A. At Brooklyn Law School she was an editor on the Brooklyn Law Review. *After being mentored by Howard Squadron, Louis Nizer, and Julia Perles, Harriet founded her own law firm, where she has represented celebrities, such as Tom Brady, Laurence Fishburne, Linda Lavin, Ute Lemper, Andrew Cuomo, Amy Lumet, Av Westin, Ann Dexter-Jones, the wives of the Weinstein brothers (Harvey and Bob), and the two moms who are the subject of Harriet's piece presented here. Harriet's law firm, Cohen Stine Kapoor LLP, is one of the top matrimonial law firms in New York. Harriet has been named to the Super Lawyers list of top New York Metropolitan Area attorneys for over a decade, and to the list of Top 50 Women Lawyers in the Metropolitan Area, and Top 100 Lawyers in the Metropolitan Area, for as long. Brooklyn Law School honored Harriet as its "Alumna of the Year," in February 2020. In 2023, Harriet was selected for the Crain's list of New York's Notable Women in*

Law. The following essay is an excerpt from her forthcoming mem-oir of her life in the law.

It was Friday, August 9, 1991. I received a telephone call from a frantic woman named Sandra Russo, herself a lawyer. She told me her family was being threatened with legal jeopardy. And that she had been told, "You need Harriet Cohen."

Russo's life partner, Robin Young, had been served with a lawsuit by Thomas Steele, a gay man from San Francisco, also a lawyer, who was the sperm donor with whose sperm, collected in an artichoke jar, Robin had been inseminated. Tom's lawsuit demanded custody of the product of that insemination, the women's nine-year old daughter, Ry Russo-Young.

Tom's lawsuit demanded immediate interim relief—a court order directing Robin to turn the child over to Tom before the end of August and over the Labor Day Weekend, so he could fly with her from New York to California—without her sister and without her mothers—to meet his family. His demands were bone-chilling to Russo and Robin.

Written contracts were not an option when Robin and Russo made the handshake deal in the early 80s with two gay men, Tom Steele and Jack Kolb, to deliver their sperm to the women and only make themselves known to the children conceived in this manner at such time as the children might start to ask, "Who is my daddy?" There were to be no other obligations or rights for the men, and their relationship with the two girls would be as "the men who helped make them" but not as their fathers.

The story of the litigation became the story of my life for the next four years—1991–1995, and the story of my case of a lifetime. Not only of my lifetime, but also of nine-year old Ry's. She was no passive observer.

Given the time pressure, I asked them both to come to the office later that afternoon for a full discussion and to bring with them a copy of the lawsuit and any documents they thought might be important. They arrived several hours later, bringing with them their two daughters, Cade and Ry.

I had to be very careful with interactions I might have with Ry, so as not to create any conflicts either for myself or for the child. Ry was a minor, and the court would soon appoint an attorney, what was then called a Law Guardian, to represent her interests. I was going to represent her mother, and the law did not assume that the interests of mother and child were, necessarily, the same.

This is what Sandra Russo and Robin Young told me that day in my office:

In 1979, Russo was thirty-nine years old, Robin was twenty-four. They lived together in a West Village apartment in a committed relationship. They both wanted kids, but as a gay couple they believed it was just something they had to give up.

But a pamphlet they read, "Women Controlled Conception," suggested otherwise. Illustrated through simple text and even simpler pictures, it showed how a woman might self-impregnate herself, using donated sperm—and a turkey baster. Neither woman had ever considered this, but the more they thought it through, the more real it seemed. And because it now seemed real, they discussed in detail exactly what they wanted to do and how they would go about doing it.

They wanted what Robin called "a traditional family." Their

idea was that each woman would be artificially inseminated by the sperm of a different donor and the children would be raised together as siblings, the offspring of both women. From the very beginning, the idea was that they would create a family, their family—and they wanted to find donors who lived far enough away from them and were not related to each other so that "part of the family" would not be an option.

Because Russo was older, thus under more biological pressure, she would become pregnant first. If everything worked out as they hoped, Robin would be pregnant next and stay home with the two children as primary caregiver. Russo would be the breadwinner.

They identified two male candidates and told each man, "This will be our family, not yours. You will have no responsibilities and no rights. Eventually, if the child asks to see you, you will make yourself available, as per our instructions."

The first sperm donor ejaculated into a jar—one that had formerly held artichoke hearts. They put the jar in a paper bag to keep it away from direct light, as the pamphlet recommended. Later that day, Russo was impregnated—with a glass syringe, a turkey baster. Nine months later, their daughter Cade Russo-Young was born.

The second sperm donor did the same. Robin used Steele's sperm. Tom, thirty-one years old, was a well-known attorney. He was intelligent and handsome.

She spelled out their conditions—"no rights, no responsibilities"—and he offered oral assurances that he understood and agreed to those terms.

At the time of the visit, a man was staying with Tom, whom

Russo and Robin referred to as "the Sailor," because his manner or his dress put them in mind of something nautical. They never knew his name.

Tom and the Sailor went upstairs and shortly afterwards both came down. Tom handed Robin an artichoke jar with his sperm. Robin used the turkey baster.

Ry Russo-Young was born on November 16, 1981. For the next four years, there was no contact of any kind between the mothers and the donors.

The women had always expected that sooner or later Cade and Ry would start asking questions about their circumstances, why they had two mothers, and other matters, but they assumed it would be later—perhaps in junior high school. Instead, in 1985, when five-year-old Cade began attending pre-school, she came home one day and said that all her classmates had been talking about their fathers . . . where was hers?

Russo and Robin told me they had always determined to be honest with the girls, and to treat them equally, as sisters; so, even though at this time only Cade was curious, they spoke to them both, providing a simple explanation about what happened. Cade remained curious about her "father," wondering if she would ever see him. At this point, the mothers contacted both men, asking if they would be willing to meet with the children. They agreed, and Russo and Robin told Cade and Ry they were all going to San Francisco to see "the men who helped make you."

The first meeting—Jack, Tom, Russo, Robin, Cade, and Ry— went very well; Russo said there was a wonderful, generous spirit about it, and Robin "felt so thankful to these guys." A pattern developed. The mothers and daughters visited with the donors once or twice a year, during school vacations, spending summers together, renting a beach house. The men were expected to treat the children as if they were biological sisters, not to favor one over the other and not to assume any stronger bond existed with one of the girls. The men never saw the children except in the company of the mothers, Russo and Robin said, and they were treated as good family friends. All seemed happy with the arrangement.

Over time, Jack stopped coming. But the relationship with Tom deepened. They saw him not only on vacation or during the summer but when he came to the city on business. During those times, he would sometimes stay in their West Village apartment and, occasionally, attend school events for the girls.

As the years went by, it became apparent to Russo and Robin—and, most probably, they said, to Cade—that although Tom may have tried to treat each of the girls equally, it didn't come naturally to him, and he was developing a special fondness for Ry. That worried them and created some tension among the adults.

That tension increased when Tom began a relationship with a man named Milton who would become his life partner. The relationship Russo and Robin had built with Tom was, by its nature, somewhat delicate and required a sense of discretion and mutual understanding. Milton either didn't understand or didn't respect the dynamic they had worked to create. He encouraged Ry to refer to Tom as "Daddy" and to the women, it was clear that he had no respect for the boundaries they had set. Eventually they told Tom: We don't want Milton around our children.

Tom thereafter did come to visit with them—alone—in

New York, but it was stressful, and he had as little interaction with Russo and Robin as possible. A series of angry letters were exchanged, the women accusing Tom of trying to undo their original agreement, Tom saying they had all changed over the years and that a new understanding was inevitable. He complained that the women were trying to control his relationship with Ry, afraid of, in words, "the love between a father and his daughter." The mothers grew very worried.

Matters came to a head when Tom told Russo and Robin he wanted to take Ry and Cade to a Steele family celebration in California at the end of August 1991. The mothers were not invited. It unsettled them that Tom would even consider this—he hadn't yet told his family that he had a daughter, and told Russo and Robin he wasn't sure how he'd manage this. The women flatly refused to allow their children to attend unaccompanied by their mothers. Tom said he was fed up with their preventing him from spending time with the girls alone, or with his family.

The women thought that the three of them were still trying to work things out, so the lawsuit came as a bolt from the blue. Tom had given no indication he was preparing to go to court.

The mothers brought a copy of the lawsuit to my office. It had been filed on Monday, August 5th, 1991 against Robin Young, and was served on her August 8. Russo was not named, as she had no blood relation to Robin or Ry. Tom would come to insist that Russo not be permitted into the courtroom during the trial.

The lawsuit asked the court to issue a declaration of paternity and recognize Tom as Ry's father, which obviously raised potential questions of custody. It further asked the court to permit "liberal and unsupervised visitation between [Steele] and his daughter Ry." And it sought an order compelling Robin to produce Ry immediately so that Tom could take her to California for several weeks.

Both women felt betrayed. They thought Tom filed suit because he assumed that they would not fight to protect the family they had put together.

At this point, Russo called me and, as recounted, I met with her and Robin that same day.

I had found both women very impressive during that initial meeting, and that impression strengthened as the case progressed. They were intelligent and keenly able to understand the fight they were conducting, the stakes involved, and what they would have to do to prevail. They were clear about what they wanted—that Tom never be granted parental rights and never be legally recognized as Ry's father. They trusted each other completely, understood, and never deviated from their goal.

And they trusted me. I don't remember a single disagreement about strategy—and that is unusual in a case so difficult and controversial. So, I was able to develop and pursue a supple and powerful strategy to achieve their objectives.

There was yet another factor of some importance to the case. I liked both women. I tend to identify with my clients and in this case, I genuinely admired Russo and Robin and the life they had built for themselves. It had not been easy, but they had conducted themselves, as far as I could tell, with courage and, in terms of their relationship with Tom, with honor.

Our first consultation had lasted for hours, as we spoke and worked our way through the documents they had brought. It seemed to me they were making every effort to be as clear as possible, not to sugarcoat anything, to present the decision and choices they had made—good and bad, helpful to the case or unhelpful—as honestly as they could.

Russo was more direct, more forthright, her language colorful—peppered with "f..k this" or "that f..ker." She was short and seemingly pugnacious. In some ways, she reminded me of a Dead-End Kid—forever looking for a fight, never looking to end one. But she possessed a great sense of humor, a fine, analytical mind and was, notwithstanding her public persona, a woman of great kindness and sensitivity.

Robin, younger by fifteen years, was more reserved, quieter, and seemingly more measured. But in the brief time we spent together, I recognized that she possessed, as they say, a will of iron; that she was, in her way, as tough and determined as Russo.

One of the important factors in our favor was that Tom and his attorney completely misread Robin, underestimating her and her fierce desire to protect her daughters and the family they had built around them. Tom and his lawyers apparently believed that by removing Russo from the legal equation, they had significantly reduced the power, purpose, and will of Robin's side. They were wrong. Everyone could see how tough Russo was. It took a keener eye to recognize those same qualities in Robin, but they were there.

Russo and Robin told me that the girls understood what was happening, believed they had two parents—the mothers—and that Tom represented a threat to a life they valued. They seemed extremely well-adjusted, well-loved, and very close to each other. They weren't paralyzed by what was happening their mothers told me. They went to school, played with friends, lived, as much as possible, the life young girls lived. Inevitably, some of this changed as the trial progressed, but based on what the mothers and the girls' attorney told me, they were doing well. They also told me Ry thought of me as her hero.

When I evaluated the case, as I then understood it, there were a number of factors that seemed to favor our position.

The most important were the women themselves. Russo and Robin were in a stable, loving relationship and they had created a stable, loving family. We might present that family to the judge as a *fait accompli* and a *mise-en-scéne* of domestic security and affection—two parents, a breadwinner and a stay-at-home mom, two children—that the judge would be loath to tamper with or alter in any way. He had enormous power to preserve this reality—or destroy it.

I already knew, at this very early stage, that it would be important to see this family as real, for us to present it to him as real—in a sense, upping the ante. If he ruled for Tom, he would be tearing this beautiful thing apart. In addition, the close, loving relationship between Cade and Ry was an essential positive factor. Judges are traditionally ill-disposed to separate or upset the relationship of siblings,

Tom was now claiming that Ry was his daughter and that he loved her as a daughter. But there was the uncontested fact that for the first four years of her life, he had had no contact with her and made no effort to contact her or have any relationship with her. He had displayed indifference to her very existence, and it was Robin and Russo who had initiated contact and encouraged a relationship, acting, as they always did, in the best interests of their children. The terms of that relationship had been spelled out and agreed to by both parties.

In essence, they had a contract—an oral contract. Robin and Russo had fulfilled their part of the bargain; it was Tom who was in default. In one of the documents the women gave me, a letter Tom wrote to Russo, he seemed to acknowledge their understanding regarding Ry and how she would be raised, while at the same time insisting on how the terms must now be changed.

Of equal if not paramount importance, although Tom came from a wealthy family, he had never been asked to contribute—and indeed had never contributed any money to the family or, more significantly, to Ry's upbringing. Not a penny.

The law is very much about encouraging someone who wants to take responsibility as a father. The state wants to ensure that the child is provided for and does not end up on the public dole. In this case, it was our job to persuade the judge that this was not a possibility because the mothers had sufficient means.

Finally, Ry herself was certainly going to be a key part of our legal effort. Much would depend on whom the court would choose to represent her interests. We hoped the Law Guardian would be sympathetic to our arguments and, most importantly, sympathetic to the child herself. The mothers assured me in that first meeting that Ry was unusually mature, that, in their words, "she knew her own mind." But exactly what weight the court would put on a nine-year-old's thinking, how it would evaluate her stated wishes and preferences would be determined largely by the heart and soul of various other players—the court-appointed Law Guardian, the psychiatrist appointed by the court to evaluate Ry, the parties, and the judge himself. At this early stage of the case, with so many unknowns, the one I had confidence in was Ry.

There was one other factor that played into my thinking those first days, a very personal one. This was the case of a lifetime. I'd known that from the first moment Russo called and asked for my help. I was an attorney specializing in family law and here was an opportunity to change or at the least expand the definition of "family" in an important and positive way. It was the type of case that made a life in the law meaningful, and it was possible that the outcome might not only provide relief to my clients but also provide legal protection and safety to others across the country as they struggled to create new families, new connections, based on new, or perhaps newly acknowledged, realities.

And I believed one other thing: it was not beyond the realm of possibility that we could lose. We faced an inhospitable legal landscape:

Courts did not then protect or even acknowledge the rights of lesbian couples. New York State's system of jurisprudence and the larger legal environment were unsympathetic to our arguments.

The idea that a couple might consciously create a family in which children were parented by two women was largely incomprehensible under prevailing principles of family law. Or the judge could exercise his power to make this a three-parent family.

We were in legal limbo. New York State would not let the mothers marry or permit them to adopt the girls. The rights routinely granted to heterosexual couples were denied them because they were lesbians. And the courts acted from the assumption that the traditional nuclear family was obviously, by its nature, in the best interests of the children.

Being a parent is a legal status, subject to interpretation by each state's laws, but there wasn't at this time a state in the Union whose laws defining and governing parenthood did not reflect the idea that "biology is destiny." Legal reforms would not take hold for another decade or more.

Robin and Russo realized they faced peculiar legal and social vulnerabilities. But all four of them thought that what they were doing was no one's business but their own. In a way, they saw themselves as pioneers, with shared interests, operating through faith and trust, beyond the boundaries of law and custom. They knew that children of lesbians were regularly removed from their custody.

We would be arguing that Robin and Tom had, in essence, a contract. But as nothing had been written down, Tom might deny there was an agreement or claim that his understanding of any agreement was different, and that he never would have agreed to the terms Robin specified. As is said, in court "an oral agreement isn't worth the paper it's written on."

Even more problematic was the fact that Robin and Russo had brought this on themselves. It was they who had invited Tom into their family—for reasons that were completely understandable, even laudable—and they had established a relationship with him and permitted their children to establish a relationship, of some intimacy, with him. The documents and photos the mothers had brought to my office evidenced all that, and I had to assume that Tom's legal team possessed similar documentation of their relationships. In addition, the mothers had permitted Tom to stay in their apartment. So, there would be no denying the fact that an affectionate relationship of some type existed or, we would argue, had existed, between Tom and Ry; but the exact nature of that relationship would be determined by the court.

Tom argued in his filing that his connection with Ry was not only biological, but emotional: he loved her as a daughter and, more importantly, he claimed that was how Ry thought of him. He said that when he arrived at their apartment, Ry would shout "Daddy's here." The mothers denied this. They had told me that Ry thought of Tom, and treated Tom, as a close family friend. And they said there was no emotional confusion: Ry knew who Tom was, and knew who her parents were—Robin and Russo.

That first weekend, I was most concerned with the tremendous time constraint we were under. We wanted to file our response to Tom's lawsuit when court opened on Monday morning because he and his team were asking for immediate interim relief that would allow Tom to take Ry to California. This was completely unacceptable to Robin and Russo, and I believed that to permit Tom to take Ry would be an assertion of privilege that could do terrific damage to our case. The pressure we were under was extraordinary, but we had to respond quickly and forcefully to let Tom's team know that they were in for a fight.

Our initial filing had to accomplish a number of goals. The Family Court judge who would be hearing the case was Edward M. Kaufmann. All I knew about him at the time was that he was a respected jurist with a reputation for intelligence and being fairminded. I was counting on the latter, because there was absolutely no settled case law that supported our position.

I was taught by my mentor, Louis Nizer, that the last paragraph of your brief, your strongest, should really be your first paragraph. You wanted to make it as easy as possible for the judge to understand your argument, if not to sympathize with that argument.

I wrote the papers that weekend and in the first paragraph we disputed every assertion made by the opposition. It was, I believed, as powerful an argument as I was capable of making in this first filing. But reading it over, I believed it wasn't enough. We had to find a way to slow the process down.

Tom was claiming to be Ry's father . . . based on what? Let him prove it. There was nothing written down, no order of filiation, his name was not on the birth certificate. There was simply no reason why we had to accept Tom's claim. And there was the question of the Sailor—who had gone upstairs with Tom. Who could say that the semen the women had been given wasn't the Sailor's?

That was the relief we requested in our filing: ". . . an order requiring the mother, the child and the alleged father to submit to blood grouping tests . . .." Tom was reportedly furious.

Mr. Nizer taught me "Hardheaded is soft hearted." He meant that you often have to make very difficult decisions on behalf of your client, decisions that may adversely affect your client in the short run, in order to secure their objectives in the long run. It was never a matter of wanting to stick a needle in Ry's arm or wanting her to be in court. And there were times, understandably, when Ry was upset, even scared. She knew she was at the center of a bitter legal battle, but she remained determined to have her voice heard. Every strategic decision we made came only after consultation with Robin and Russo; and the well-being of Ry and Cade and the survival of their family was always uppermost in their minds.

They were worried that Tom might follow Ry on the street or come to her school. They changed their phone number and unlisted it. They notified the school of their concern and left Tom's picture with the guards: Don't let this man near Ry; don't let Ry go home with anyone but us. This was the atmosphere in which we were preparing our case.

I believed that when Judge Kaufmann approved my motion and ordered the requested blood tests, he sent a signal of open-mindedness. Court is always a crapshoot and much depends on the experience, temperament, intelligence—even the mood of the judge. The more I learned about Judge Kaufmann, the more impressed I became and the more confident that, if we did go to trial, we would receive a fair hearing.

The summer waned. The blood tests came back confirming Tom as Ry's biological father. But we had bought time on a good faith basis that we needed to prepare ourselves for a very complicated and emotional trial. It started in March 1992 and, after seven long months, ended in October 1992.

After the trial ended, we just waited and waited for the judge's ruling. Ry and Cade went to school. Russo went back to work. Robin continued to manage their home. Months passed. The judge was giving this consequential case the care and deliberation that was its due.

On Tuesday, April 13, 1993, I finally received the decision:

Thomas S. apparently believes that Ry, as his biological child, must feel fatherly affection for him. He is incorrect, I think. Ry has been brought up to view Robin Y. and Sandra R. as equal mothers raising two children, and to view Thomas S. as an important man in her family's life. In her family, there has been no father. Robin Y. and Sandra R. are deeply committed to this concept of their family and Ry, who has been raised by them, must also be committed to the concept at this point in her life . . . Ry considers Sandra R. and Robin Y. to be her parents and Cade to be her full sister. She understands the underlying biological relationships, but they are not the reality of her life. The reality of her life is having two mothers, Robin Y. and Sandra R., working together to raise her and her sister. Ry does not now and has never viewed Thomas S. as a functional third parent . . . Ry . . . views this court proceeding as an attack on and threat to her positive image of herself and her family. Her sense of family security is threatened. She has expressed fear of ongoing court involvement and worries about a confusing and threatening period in her family's life. She fears that Thomas S. might seek custody of her. . . . For her, a declaration of paternity would be a statement that her family is other than she knows it to be and needs it to be. A declaration of paternity naming Thomas S. as Ry's father, under the circumstances at this late time in her life, would not be in her best interests. Even were there an adjudication of paternity, I would deny Thomas S.'s application for visitation. . . . Accordingly, the proceeding is dismissed.

I couldn't reach Robin, but Russo was at her desk and picked up the phone. "We won," I said.

Ry grew up to become a filmmaker. She made a documentary about the case that was featured on HBO Prime in 2022 called "Nuclear Family." Ry interviewed me and examined my strategies and our joys and sorrows under a microscope. She examined Tom's motives. "What was Tom looking for?" somebody asks in the film. "But he had that already," the questioner concludes in the documentary.

Two things stand out for me. Russo's words to me in our first phone call. "You need Harriet Cohen." And, "but he had that already."

Tom died from complications of AIDS in 1998.

18

The Cost of Winning

by Dean Martha Minow

Martha Minow graduated from the University of Michigan, earned a master's degree from Harvard, and earned a J.D. degree from the Yale Law School. She clerked first for Judge David Bazelon on the U.S. Court of Appeals for the District of Columbia Circuit and then for Supreme Court Justice Thurgood Marshall. She has been a member of the Harvard Law School faculty since 1981 and served as Dean of the Law School. Her most recent book is Saving the News: Why the Constitution Calls for a Government Action to Preserve Freedom of Speech. *She continues to engage in pro bono litigation and also serves on the boards of nonprofit organizations and foundations. She first encountered* Walker v. Birmingham, *the case that prompted the litigation discussed in her essay, while a student in Professor Owen Fiss's course on Injunctions at the Yale Law School in 1979.*

Justice and common sense should prevail, but technicalities and niceties often prevent the right result. This is true sometimes even when people overcome the obstacles to explaining the full situation to those in a position to do something about it. I learned this lesson more than once during law school.

The prime example was the Supreme Court's rejection of Dr. Martin Luther King, Jr.'s efforts to overturn the contempt order sending him to the Birmingham, Alabama jail where he wrote his searing, "Letter from a Birmingham Jail." Years later, I had the chance, in another case, to confront the same technical issue I thought the Supreme Court had wrongly decided in Dr. King's case. It is called the "Collateral Bar Rule." And, in that later case, while I knew a lot about that rule, I still had a lot to learn about what a lawyer owes the clients.

The Supreme Court's treatment of Dr. King arose after courageous civil rights activists pursued peaceful civil disobedience to challenge the pervasive regime of white supremacy governing the city's commercial and social worlds, law enforcement, and courts. As Professor Randall Kennedy later described it (in the 2017 Supreme Court Review):

> Eating establishments were racially segregated, as were drinking fountains, dressing rooms, bathrooms, elevators, taxis, ambulances, and hotels. It was a crime for blacks and whites to play cards, checkers, or dice with one another. When a court ordered the desegregation of the city's recreation facilities, the municipal government closed them all—sixty-eight parks, thirty-eight playgrounds, six swimming pools, and four golf courses.

City law enforcement officers arrested activist protestors involved in boycotts, marches, and sit-ins. Then the city officials sought and obtained in an ex parte hearing (a hearing where only the city officials were in court with the judge) a temporary restraining order. This order enjoined the two leading organizations and 139 named individuals, including Dr. King, from participating in or encouraging "mass processions or like demonstrations" without a permit as required by a city ordinance. This restraining order was delivered just before Good Friday, when Dr. King and his colleagues were planning a march against Jim Crow laws.

Dr. King and his colleagues explained publicly that in the past, they had "abided by federal injunctions out of respect for the forthright and consistent leadership that the federal judiciary has given in establishing the principle of integration as the law of the land," but they believed that the recalcitrant forces in the Birmingham community would use the courts "to perpetuate the unjust and illegal system of racial separation" as an "unjust, undemocratic and unconstitutional misuse of the judicial process" (quoting the Supreme Court's decision in *Walker v. City of Birmingham* in 1967).

The group's prior application for permits had been summarily denied. Indeed, Commissioner of Public Safety Bull Connor had previously told them, "No, you will not get a permit in Birmingham, Alabama to picket. I will picket you to the city jail" (quoting *Walker*).

The activists decided not to delay their march with an appeal to the Birmingham court because Dr. King's prior civil rights mobilization effort in Albany, Georgia fell apart when the leaders waited for the judicial process to work through a similar set of issues (King Encyclopedia, The Albany Movement).

So, the marchers disobeyed the injunction in Birmingham. They were arrested. And they learned that they had lost the right to contest the legality of the injunction.

A court-made rule—the "Collateral Bar Rule"—directs people to bring their concerns and objections first to the court that had issued the injunction rather than disobey it and then raise objections in their defense to charges of criminal contempt of court. To this day, in most U.S. courts, the rule bars any objection to such an injunction raised after it has been disobeyed.

Hence the courts treat judicial orders differently from acts of the legislature or any other government officials. People are allowed to raise any and all concerns in their defense after disobeying a legal rule, whether a speeding ticket, or statute criminalizing certain conduct. The Collateral Bar Rule makes judicial orders uniquely unavailable to legal challenges, including constitutional challenges, unless obeyed prior to raising objections.

Declining to wait for what would no doubt be a futile court challenge to the restraining order, some fifty activists proceeded to march as a crowd of approximately 1,500 watched. Dr. King and his colleagues were charged with contempt. The Supreme Court of Alabama affirmed with exceptions only where proof of participation in the march was lacking.

After serving his five-day jail term, Reverend King and his colleagues pursued review in the U.S. Supreme Court. And it was the Supreme Court's decision reached several years later in the case named *Walker v. City of Birmingham* that seemed—and seems—to me to compound the injustices at work there in Birmingham.

The Supreme Court's majority of five justices criticized the activists for failing to take any steps to challenge the lawfulness of the injunction before they disobeyed it. And they also reasoned that this was "not a case where the injunction was transparently invalid or had only a frivolous pretense to validity." What could have been a more transparently invalid injunction than an ex parte order preventing a peaceful protest to individuals who had been resolutely denied permits to protest? This is the question pointedly raised by the Justices who dissented, in opinions by Chief Justice Earl Warren and Justice William Brennan.

Ever since I started teaching law students, I regularly include the Supreme Court's decision in my civil procedure materials. I also have given students Dr. King's "Letter from a Birmingham Jail," which explains the reasons for protests and for civil disobedience. There, Dr. King wrote in response to a public statement by eight white clergymen urging the activists and members of the Black community to use the courts and not the streets to secure civil rights. Dr. King responded:

> For years now I have heard the word "wait!" It rings in the ear of every Negro with a piercing familiarity. This "wait'" has almost always meant never . . . We must come to see with the distinguished jurist of yesterday that "justice too long delayed is justice denied." We have waited for more than 340 years for our constitutional and God-given rights.

I have invited students to consider the justifications for the Collateral Bar Rule. But I have never accepted its application in a case where the underlying injunction so patently relies on an unconstitutional law. Such obvious unconstitutionality was present in Dr. King's case. The Supreme Court itself rejected as unconstitutional the ordinance underlying the injunction that Dr. King disobeyed. The Court explained that the ordinance unacceptably gave unlimited discretion to local law-enforcement officials to deny parade permits and, hence, impermissibly consigned constitutionally protected and lawful freedom of expression to the whim and prejudices of local officials

Eight years after I started teaching, my phone rang and lawyers at the American Civil Liberties Union asked, "How would you like to help with a lawsuit challenging the application of the Collateral Bar Rule? The case arose in connection with the publication by the *Providence Journal* of an article about the death of Raymond L. S. Patriarca—the alleged leader of an organized crime family. The article included information the *Journal* secured from the FBI under the Freedom of Information Act. The FBI turned the material over to the *Journal* and other news outlets, even though the FBI surveillance itself had been previously ruled unlawful.

Raymond J. Patriarca, the deceased's son, sued both the *Journal* and the FBI to enjoin publication. His suit asserted that the *Journal* had violated federal statutes and the Constitution. A day after service of the complaint, the District Court held a hearing about whether to issue a restraining order or injunction. There, the *Journal* argued that blocking publication of materials from illegal surveillance was a prior restraint in direct violation of the First Amendment's guarantees of freedom of speech and the press.

Right after the hearing, the District Court issued a temporary restraining order and scheduled a further hearing for a few days later. Not waiting for that hearing, the *Journal* on the day after the initial hearing, published an article about the deceased Patriarca and included information taken from the FBI logs and memoranda. The son, Raymond, immediately moved to hold the *Journal* and its executive editor in contempt of court.

The District Court appointed a special prosecutor to present the argument in a hearing on the motion and then found the *Journal* guilty of criminal contempt. The judge imposed an eighteen-month jail term on the executive editor, suspended that sentence pending performance of 200 hours of public service, and fined the Journal $100,000.

The *Journal* on appeal to the First Circuit Court of Appeals argued that the order was an unconstitutional prior restraint of speech. Very much like Dr. King, the *Journal* faced the Collateral Bar Rule. If applied to our case, the rule would prevent the appellate court from considering the constitutionality of the underlying restraining order.

The appeal was initially heard by the usual three-judge court and it issued an opinion written by Judge John Minor Wisdom, a distinguished senior judge who was designated to spend time on the First Circuit. His opinion for the panel stressed that a prior restraint of speech must be presumptively unconstitutional and only the most serious government interests can override that presumption; at the same time, the opinion describes as "well-established" in a civilized government the rule that a party subject to the jurisdiction of the court must obey a court order or else face criminal contempt. With quite a detailed discussion of *Walker v. City of Birmingham*, Judge Wisdom for the court concluded that court orders, however important, are not sacrosanct. And using the reasoning of the Supreme Court in *Walker,* Judge Wisdom concluded that a "transparently invalid order cannot form the basis for a contempt citation."

All six permanent judges of the First Circuit then decided to hear the case. Sitting "en banc," the court summarily modified Judge Wisdom's opinion for the three-judge panel, holding that even those subject to a transparently invalid order must make a good faith effort to seek emergency appellate relief. At the same time, the court clarified that the publisher may proceed to publish and challenge the constitutionality of the order in the contempt proceeding if timely access to the appellate court is not available or if a timely decision is not forthcoming.

In our case, the five members of the court were not convinced that the *Journal* could have obtained emergency relief before needing to decide whether to run the story the following day, and further concluded it would be unfair to subject the *Journal* and its executive editor to substantial sanctions for failing to follow procedures that after all were announced after the events at issue. The court indicated that henceforth, a party facing what it believes to be a transparently invalid order needs to undertake at least a good faith effort to raise the objections in court before violating the order. One judge on the en banc panel disagreed with the majority and instead called for new briefing and a hearing. By a margin of 5–1, the en banc court left in place the three-judge panel's decision that had overturned the contempt ruling.

Mr. Patriarca took the case to the Supreme Court. I proudly submitted a brief in that court.

After a few weeks, my phone rang again with a further call about the case. This time the call was from Floyd Abrams, a leading First Amendment lawyer who was representing the *Journal*. He said he had detected a procedural problem that would allow the Supreme Court to dismiss Patriarca's case altogether.

The United States Attorney who ordinarily would enforce the District Court's contempt citation could not do so in this case because of his role in another case. The District Court accordingly appointed a special prosecutor. The special prosecutor asked the Solicitor General, the top Justice Department lawyer responsible for representing the federal government in the Supreme Court, to authorize him to proceed with the case. The Solicitor General denied this request.

Floyd said that without that approval, the case could not proceed at the Supreme Court. I started to object: "but then we can't get the Supreme Court to review our argument about the Collateral Bar Rule." I so wanted to vindicate not only freedom of speech and expose a transparently invalid court order—I wanted the Supreme Court to revisit the Collateral Bar Rule and its treatment of Dr. King.

Floyd was patient with me with a reminder I remember to this day. He stressed that the *Journal* had won in the Court of Appeals; it had avoided contempt. The *Journal* could keep its victory if the Supreme Court dismissed the case. My dreams of fighting injustice came face-to-face with actual results for the actual litigant in the case.

Floyd proceeded with his argument based on the technicality and prevailed. The Supreme Court did not, however, simply dismiss the case. Instead, it produced a substantial opinion explaining why the consent of the Solicitor General was especially relevant. In an opinion by Justice Harry Blackmun, the Court supplied a learned discussion of the role of the Solicitor General in varied circumstances involving a court-appointed prosecutor addressing contempt of court issues. It interpreted statutes, prior case law, and policies. And then it dismissed the case.

This was not the opinion of my hopes. But it was sufficient as a victory for the *Journal*. And I learned a critical lesson about lawyering: it is about real clients, with real issues, not just principles divorced from effects in the world. Challenging the "Collateral Bar Rule" and vindicating Dr. King would have to wait for another day.

19

Silence is Golden

by Michael Helfer

Michael Helfer graduated from Claremont Men's College and the Harvard Law School. He clerked for Chief Judge David Bazelon on the U.S. Court of Appeals for the District of Columbia Circuit. Michael was a partner at WilmerHale where we met, and he served as the firm's chairman for several years. Thereafter, Michael joined Nationwide Insurance as President of Strategic Investments and Chief Strategic Officer. Michael then joined Citigroup where he became Secretary and General Counsel and then Vice Chairman.

Two of my most successful and professionally rewarding legal experiences involved my going to court and saying almost nothing. That is a strategy that would likely horrify most courtroom lawyers and, to be clear, it is only seldom my strategy. But there is a time and place for it.

The first occasion was a pro bono representation of a foster mother—call her Mrs. X. She and her husband had taken in a baby boy as a foster child and received payments from the District of Columbia government to offset the costs involved. When I got involved, the boy was thirteen years old. In the interim,

Mrs. X's husband had died. Mrs. X wanted to keep the boy—who called her "mother"—but she could not afford to care for him without the foster care payments. At that time, District regulations provided that a teenage male's foster home had to include an adult male. For this reason, the District government came to take the boy away from Mrs. X. We were asked by a child-advocacy non-profit to represent the mother on a pro bono basis.

We immediately sought an injunction—a court order—that would stop the District from taking the boy away from Mrs. X. And we filed a brief in support of our position. The court scheduled a hearing to consider the injunction request. At the hearing, the District was represented by a nice, but very inexperienced lawyer. The court had appointed a lawyer to represent the boy and he aligned with us because the boy wanted to stay with Mrs. X. And I was there—having assiduously prepared to argue our case.

The judge took the bench and said: "I have read the briefs. I don't need to hear from the boy's counsel or the foster mother's counsel. What I want to know is whether the District will let the boy stay with his foster mother, or do I have to issue an injunction?" The young lawyer representing the District started to read the District's regulation to the Judge. The Judge interrupted, told him to sit down, and issued the injunction. We all stood up as the Judge left the bench. I had not said a word and won the case. But I never got to give the oral argument I had so diligently prepared. (Well, to be fair, I had filed a very persuasive brief.)

The second instance was in quite a different and less emotionally satisfying context—a battle between the banking and securities industries. The Federal Reserve had granted an application from our bank client to engage in certain securities activities. The securities industry sued seeking a decision that would overturn the Fed's ruling. We participated in the litigation as an intervenor on the side of the Fed.

The case was to be argued before a three-judge panel of the United States Court of Appeals for the District of Columbia Circuit. Once again, I prepared assiduously for the argument I was to present on behalf of our banking clients. At the oral argument, the very able lawyer for the securities industry went first and was brutally beaten up by the judicial panel. The Fed's lawyer then argued for only a couple of minutes. When it was my turn, sensing that the court was with us, I stood and said: "I will be happy to answer any questions the court has, but otherwise we submit the case on the briefs and the arguments made today." There were no questions, so I sat down, once again, without giving the argument I had worked so hard to prepare.

Walking out of the courtroom, the General Counsel of our client said, I think half-jokingly, "I assume you are not going to bill us since you did not make an argument." I replied: "It is harder to decide not to argue than to argue, so I will bill you double." He laughed. We won.

20

The Law as Cross-Cultural Adventure

by Warren Cooke

Warren Cooke graduated from Dartmouth College and the Yale Law School. He spent his entire career specializing in international transactions and corporate law at Milbank Tweed Hadley & McCloy in New York and Hong Kong. Warren is an accomplished pianist and an uncommonly talented birder and bird photographer.

"This is what I want to be doing."

I thought those words, maybe I spoke them, as the West Coast of Africa came into view from our Pan Am prop plane on New Years Day, 1974.

I was on my way to Kinshasa, the capital of the Republic of Zaire (previously the Belgian Congo and today called the Democratic Republic of the Congo) to represent that country in the financing of a major infrastructure project: the proposed Inga-Shaba power transmission line.

The country—the second largest in Africa—had become independent only in 1960, and had acquired the name "Zaire" in 1965 when Mobutu Sese Seko seized power and became president.

I had gone to law school in considerable part out of an interest in international affairs and international law. I had exchange student experience at Dartmouth College, and before law school, I had been a U.S. State Department interpreter, French-English / English-French. (French was one of the four official languages of Zaire). At Yale Law School I greatly enjoyed several international law courses with professors such as Eugene Rostow and Leon Lipson. After law school I became an associate at Milbank, Tweed, Hadley & McCloy (now simply called Milbank) in New York in the hope of becoming active in international matters. I was a sixteen-month associate there when, on New Year's Eve 1973, I set out for Zaire with a Milbank partner, the intense, brilliant and dedicated Francis D. Logan.

It was to be a cross-cultural education.

Upon arrival in Kinshasa, we checked into the Intercontinental Hotel. The hotel was situated alongside the Zaire (formerly Congo) River, a river so vast that whole islands of water-hyacinth, broken off upstream, floated past the hotel all day long. Frank expressed disappointment that none of the Zaire team was available to work with us; he saw no particular reason why one should not work on New Year's Day. He and I went ahead and worked on the deal documents until late in the evening. It was surely going to be necessary to adjust a bit from the head-down-and-charge Wall Street approach to the African timetable.

As I walked out of the hotel the next morning, I saw a flock of grey parrots in the canopy and a Pin-Tailed Whydah perched in a flowering tree; the air was a combination of floral fragrance and wood smoke; women were colorfully dressed, each in four or five different patterns; unmistakably we were in Africa. A driver was there to collect us and take us to the presidency where we marched past heavily armed guards into the antechamber attached to the office of President Mobutu. He was away (apparently at a spa in Paris), but the antechamber itself was impressive enough, with a monumental piece of polished malachite displayed on a table, like a seven-foot ashtray. We were greeted by the second most powerful figure in Zaire, Citoyen Bisengimana.

In a seemingly confused combination of rejection of European colonialism and acceptance of French (revolutionary) vocabulary, everyone in Zaire was now addressed as "Citoyen" or "Citoyenne" (Citizen), while the President was now universally referred to as "Le Guide." Colonial era place names had of course been changed so that, for example, names such as Leopoldville and Stanleyville had been changed to Kinshasa and Kisangani, respectively.

Citizen Bisengimana escorted us to a small auditorium where we addressed a group of officials about the financing with myself acting as interpreter. The reception seemed a bit frosty and suspicious at first, but I realized soon enough that the crowd was confused about our role—they heard we were from the New York offices of "Mille Banques," which is French for a thousand banks, and sounds exactly the same as the French pronunciation of "Milbank." It began to go better when that was cleared up and the audience understood we were on Zaire's side, not on the side of a thousand banks.

The project to be financed was ambitious. It involved the construction of a direct-current overhead transmission line, using technology from the Swedish company ASEA, to run 1,100 miles across Zaire, from the dams at Inga near the mouth of the Zaire River, and all the way to the province of Shaba (the former Katanga), where there were major copper and cobalt resources to be developed.

A fundamental point, which we stressed to the officials, was that the financing for the project needed to be put in place by February 14, 1974. Failing that, escalation provisions in the underlying commercial contracts between the construction consortium, led by Morrison-Knudsen International, and SNEL (Societe Nationale d'Electricite), the Zaire energy agency, would kick in, and the project could become uneconomic. Le Guide would not be pleased. We also stressed that for a financing of this importance, the lenders were requiring a decree signed by President Mobutu, approving the financing terms. We explained the roles of the Export-Import Bank of the U.S. (EXIM), which would provide export financing in accordance with its mission, and Citibank, which was taking the lead in the private piece of the financing. We had brought with us drafts of the loan documents prepared by EXIM and Citibank.

Over the next few days, I had an interesting inside view of post-independence Zaire. Among other things, it quickly became clear that although the top Zaire officials were smart and talented, they were vastly overworked and somewhat inexperienced. The pool of Zairois who were qualified to handle major initiatives like this one was small. This was because, the Zairois told me, Belgian colonial policy had sought to block their colonized people from access to higher education, except perhaps in the area of agriculture. Their experience was different, they said, from the experience of African nations colonized by the French, for example, where the colonizers sought to develop a Francophone educated elite.

In any event, besides Citoyen Bisengimana, I worked primarily with Citizen Nzeza Makunsi, a powerful, smart, and energetic official who ran SNEL, Citoyen Pembele, a presidential advisor, and Citoyen Mbenza Ngoma, who worked for SNEL and became a particularly good friend. And there were still Belgians in various important positions, the country often having no alternatives. One such Belgian was Maitre Jean Collinet, a Counseiller Juridique (legal advisor) who was very helpful to me when it came time to work on various internal closing documents.

We worked intensely over the next five days. Consistent with international financial practice, the loan agreements ran to about 120 pages. We had to explain the need for and length of the various documents, as well as most of their provisions, to Citoyens Nzeza, Pembele, Mbenza, and others. It was necessary to go back to basics in certain respects and explain some of the differences between the common law approach of England and the U.S., on the one hand, and the Civil Code approach of Europe on the other.

The unofficial French translations of the loan documents that had been prepared on behalf of Citibank, although helpful, occasionally complicated matters. For example, the enforcement clause providing that "The Republic hereby submits to the jurisdiction of the State Courts of, and the Federal courts in, the State of New York" had come out in the translation as providing in effect that Zaire submitted to the jurisdiction of all of the state courts in the U.S., as well as the federal courts in New York; it took a while to get past that.

The standard waiver of sovereign immunity in the document created much angst among the Zairois; since it was not a provision that EXIM or Citibank would give up, we had to give a virtual seminar to Citoyen Bisengimana, Maitre Collinet, and others on the international law of sovereign immunity, including the "commercial activity" exception under the "restrictive" theory of sovereign immunity (this was before the enactment in the U.S. of the Foreign Sovereign Immunities Act of 1976, which codified the restrictive theory), before Zaire could see its way to accepting it. I remember thinking that, notwithstanding the challenges, this was what I wanted to be doing as a lawyer.

In the meantime, Zaire itself was not without its excitement. On one evening, we were invited to dinner at the home of the Citibank representative, which was located thirty minutes or so outside Kinshasa. The road to his residence, we were told, had been the scene recently of a number of acts of piracy by some violent local bandits. We were provided with a car and driver to get there; the driver had been a fighter pilot and apparently his main strategy for getting to the Citibank residence safely was speed. The hair-raising drive out was accomplished without interruptions for banditry (although we did see a number of vehicles overturned in the ditches beside the road). On the way back, though, a group of men appeared in the headlights on the road; they appeared to be armed and to have set up a roadblock. We could see that our driver, cursing in colorful idiomatic French, was preparing to blast around or through the roadblocks, when, upon closer inspection, the group in the road appeared to be Zairois soldiers. We stopped and were interrogated and allowed to pass. They were there to apprehend the gang of bandits.

I wasn't so sure this was what I wanted to be doing.

During the dinner there had been some excitement as well. Apparently shortly before our arrival in Kinshasa, a swarm of unfamiliar insects had arrived there. They were red and firefly size and if you squashed them with your hand you ended up with an acidic burn. One of the guests showed us a quarter-sized burn on his neck where he had smacked one. They were being referred to around town as "acid bugs." Two were noted during the dinner walking along the edges of wine glasses, and several were on the inside of each dining room window. I never found out exactly what they were; we heard later that they disappeared from Kinshasa several days after we left town, a coincidence which seemed potentially to carry some risk to our reputation.

It was not necessary to travel far to have an encounter with nature. One evening there was a large open-air buffet dinner in the courtyard of the hotel. It was a beautiful spot at night, with searchlights aimed upwards at the lush, large-leaved flowery foliage. A waiter dropped a pan with a loud crash. The lush, large-leaved flowery foliage lifted off into the darkness. Much of what had been up there, directly above the buffet, consisted not of leaves but of huge fruit bats. We decided to dine indoors after all.

We left Kinshasa late on January 5, having accomplished a great deal in five days, but having a number of points to negotiate with the lenders. We travelled back to New York via Johannesburg, where we spent a night in the airport, and Rio de Janeiro. On the leg from Johannesburg to Rio, we had the good fortune to see the Comet Kohoutek out the left window of the plane. I had my birdwatching binoculars with me, of which the entire crew and many passengers made use while the comet was visible.

The next two weeks were spent going back and forth between New York and EXIM's offices in Washington, D.C., negotiating with EXIM's counsel (a fine lawyer and wonderful person named David Lowe) and meeting with Citibank and its lawyers, in an effort to obtain improvements in the legal terms from Zaire's point of view. A major issue was the "cross-default" clause, under which a default by Zaire or a Zaire government agency on other debt would put our loan into default. The cross-default clause is not something lenders give up easily, unless they are dealing with a Triple-A (AAA) credit; we were able to carve back the language but not eliminate it.

I headed back to Zaire on February 3 to explain the changes we had been able to obtain in the documents, and to prepare for the closing, which as noted had to occur by February 14. This time I was alone. Frank Logan and the EXIM and Citibank teams held back while I worked with the Zairois on the final negotiated terms of the agreements, and on the closing papers that the lenders would be requiring, which included a U.S.-style legal opinion from Maitre Collinet, and the decree that would be needed from Le Guide. It fell to me to design the decree, which required, among other things, introductory Swahili wording used in such decrees. I drafted the decree together with a French translation. I also had lengthy discussions in French with Maitre Collinet about the long-form English language legal opinion being something European lawyers were not familiar with.

During this period, between document sessions, I had some time for some cross-cultural experiences.

Citoyen Mbenza invited me to his home to meet his wife and four boys and to have a real Zairois lunch. I actually hated the first course, which was some sort of mashed and fermented plantain, but I managed to get it down, and keep it down, without notice; everything else about that lunch experience was delightful, including the rest of the meal as well as our hostess and the boys. I told Mbenza quite sincerely that he had a wonderful family.

On one evening, Citoyen Mbenza took me to a kind of nightclub in Kinshasa, in a shelter with a hard-packed dirt floor and an enthusiastic African clientele. The band consisted solely of drummers, and their performance—with multiple rhythms going on simultaneously and a gradually accelerating, pounding, increasingly wild beat, until listeners in the place were frantic—was utterly thrilling.

Mbenza took me to an open-air market in Kinshasa. There I bought a ceremonial beaded spear (no trouble with airport security in those days), a beautiful two-volume set of Bannerman's *The Birds of West and Equatorial Africa*, and several lengths of beautiful batik fabric, all of which my wife and I still have. Before leaving the market, I was warmly urged by Mbenza and the merchants to buy one more length of batik cloth: this one was covered with images of President Mobutu and the Zaire flag. I complied.

And one of those classic cross-cultural experiences—on our way back from the market, I saw three women coming down the dirt road, maybe forty yards ahead, dressed in brilliant colors and carrying large baskets on their heads. As I raised my camera and looked through the lens, I saw an empty dirt road. Even though I was with an African friend, all three women had instantly disappeared into the tall grass at the sight of my camera. Mbenza explained that such a reaction, though not universal, is common.

As an avid photographer, I have learned that where feasible, it is best to ask permission to photograph a person you don't know.

Meanwhile, for reasons relating to protocol and because of the crucial importance of the presidential decree, the lender team desired and planned for a formal in-person meeting with President Mobutu in Paris where the decree would be signed and delivered. So, on February 11, the lender team embarked for Paris; Citoyen Bisengimana put the decree into the hands of a courier, and put the courier on a commercial Air Zaire flight to Paris, where it would be conveyed to Le Guide. There was just enough time left for the lender team to obtain the signed decree, proceed to Kinshasa for the signing of all the rest of the documents, and complete the closing before the February 14 deadline. I returned to the hotel at around 8:00 that evening, having already set up the closing documents in a conference room at the presidency.

Then things went off the tracks.

I received an urgent call at the hotel from Citoyen Bisengimana. Le Guide, he said, was NOT at a spa in Paris after all. He was at a spa in Munich. And to make matters worse, he was planning to go from Munich to a destination unknown even to Citoyen Bisengimana. We were immediately in crisis mode.

I reviewed with Citoyen Bisengimana the significance of the February 14 deadline, and threw in the word "crise" (crisis) several times. Citoyen Bisengimana was presumably quite used to crises, and up to the task. He radioed the Air Zaire flight, which was in the air somewhere over Africa, and instructed it to divert. The plane, the courier, and its commercial passengers landed in Munich instead of Paris. He also alerted President Mobutu, who was presumably spending much of his time in hot mineral waters, to the urgency of the "crise" and the need to make himself available to the lenders. Meanwhile, of course, the lender team was in the air, well on its way to Paris. I began wondering whether I would be blamed for the misinformation as to the whereabouts of the president—awkward, rather, for a sixteen-month associate on whom a bunch of experienced bankers and lawyers were depending. Communications from Zaire were not easy in those days, and I spent several hours trying to assure that multiple telex and, as and when possible, telephone messages would get through to the lender team with the unwelcome news that upon arrival in Paris they needed to proceed immediately to Munich. I provided the details given to me by Citoyen Bisengimana as to how to get hold of President Mobutu once they got to Munich.

Happily, the team did catch up with Le Guide in Munich late on February 12 and obtained the signed decree. They then proceeded to Kinshasa where I was organizing the relevant officials for the closing ceremonies. The signing of the papers occurred at Banque du Zaire (the central bank) late on February 13 and sign-off on the remaining closing documents occurred at the presidency on the next day—February 14. I remember thinking this is what I want to be doing.

I learned a number of early lessons from the Zaire transaction. I already knew that as a lawyer engaged in the world of transactions, technical excellence, legal knowledge, and very close attention to detail are all essential. I now learned that other qualities can be extremely important, including the ability to be calm when things go awry, flexibility, organizational skill, and most assuredly inter-personal skills.

For the rest of my thirty-eight-year career at Milbank, I continued to have a variety of cross-cultural experiences, including an adventuresome stint of nine years based at the firm's Hong Kong office. The Inga-Shaba power line was completed in 1982.

21

Justice Delayed

by Roger M. Witten

In 1962, Trinidad and Tobago became an independent nation. For its first twenty-four years of independence until 1986, the People's National Movement party (PNM) was ascendant. There were, however, persistent rumors about government corruption, particularly in regard to awards of oil-drilling rights in the surrounding waters.

In 1986, the opposition party, called the National Alliance for Reconstruction, ran on an anti-corruption platform and dislodged the PNM. One of its leaders, Selwyn Richardson, became the Attorney General and Minister of Justice. He immediately began an investigation into whether an American oil company called Tesoro had—about twenty years earlier—paid a bribe to PNM officials in connection with an award to Tesoro of certain oil-drilling rights. Richardson put together a team consisting of Robert Lindquist, a forensic accountant from Canada, and our law firm.

The Trinidadians we worked with were warm and friendly. But the capital, Port-au-Spain, was not a particularly welcoming place. We always stayed at the "Upside Down Hilton"—called that because elevator level number one was the building's highest floor. We were cautioned not to leave the hotel without security.

The assignment had its practical difficulties. For example, when we met with government officials to review a detailed list of documents that we needed, we noticed that, although the government officials were pleasant, they were not taking notes. When we finished, they advised us that we were unlikely to receive the documents, because the government department in question did not have copier paper, and the apparently lone copier was in any event broken.

As our investigation proceeded, we succeeded in identifying a former expat as the likely "bag man" for the alleged Tesoro bribes. We located him in London, and he agreed to meet with us.

We met at our London office. The suspect was elderly and rather courtly and charming. At first, he dodged our questions. By the conclusion of the session, however, he essentially confirmed the truth of the allegations.

Armed with this important evidence, we sued Tesoro in federal court in New York. There were two critical issues: one, could we prove the bribe, and two, would the statute of limitations bar our claim, given that the events in question had occurred more than twenty years earlier. There were respectable arguments both ways on the limitations issue. At the first court hearing, the judge (controversially, in our opinion) ruled that the case would be split with the statute of limitations issue going to trial first. If we prevailed on that issue, there would be a second trial on the merits of the case.

Then lightning struck. We received a call out of the blue from a lawyer representing a company (call it ABCo) that had a secret plan to launch a hostile take-over bid for Tesoro. ABCo was concerned that our lawsuit, if successful, could saddle Tesoro with a possibly material liability of uncertain magnitude, which could substantially reduce Tesoro's value. ABCo proposed that we drop our lawsuit in return for a payment by ABCo to Trinidad.

Whatever the possible economic merits of this proposal turned out to be, dropping the lawsuit was a political non-starter in Trinidad. So, we had to come up with a structure that let our client "have its cake and eat it too."

Intense and highly confidential negotiations ensued—confidential because ABCo's plan to take over Tesoro was top secret. Notwithstanding this concern, the negotiations were almost scuttled when one of the players mistakenly sent a draft agreement to the wrong law firm.

In the end, we reached an agreement pursuant to which 1) ABCo agreed to immediately pay Trinidad a sizable amount, and 2) Trinidad agreed to a cap on the amount of damages it could recover in the event ABCo did acquire Tesoro. As it turned out, ABCo abandoned its takeover plans for unrelated reasons.

Along the way, we held settlement talks with Tesoro. In 1990, very hard bargaining led to an agreement that Tesoro would pay $3.3 million to Trinidad, in return for a cessation of the litigation and a general release.

This agreement was contingent on securing the approval of Trinidad's legislature. That was no minor hurdle as the public debate over whether to approve the settlement was highly politicized.

Richardson asked us to prepare a speech for the Prime Minister to use to defend the settlement in the upcoming session of the legislature. We worked in Port-au-Spain over the weekend and completed a draft on Sunday. But there weren't any staffers around who could type the speech, which was to be given the next morning. A local lawyer we were working with called his secretary at home and, fortunately, she agreed to come to the ministry to type the speech. She was generously compensated, in cash.

We accompanied Richardson to the Red House, the seat of Trinidad's legislature. We sat near the prime minister and watched the fiery debate with concern. After a great deal of speechifying, the legislature voted to approve the settlement.

Within weeks of this session of the legislature, the Red House was attacked by an armed dissident group. Some legislators were killed, others injured, and the rest held hostage for several weeks. We were very fortunate that our hearing was not scheduled for that tragic day.

Selwyn Richardson became a good friend during the ups and downs of the case. His anti-corruption stand was nothing short of heroic. Most sadly, he was later assassinated.

22

Hungry for Justice

by Mark Kessel

Mark Kessel graduated from City College of New York and Syracuse University Law School. At the start of his career, he served in the Army as a lawyer. After fulfilling his military obligations, Mark practiced corporate law while a long-time partner at Shearman & Sterling in New York and San Francisco. He has served as his firm's first managing partner. Mark also co-founded Symphony Capital, a private equity firm investing in biopharma companies. He continues to be a major presence in that industry.

In 1966, after I was admitted to the New York Bar, I was inducted as a Captain in the U.S. Army Judge Advocate General's Corps (JAG) and received orders to serve in its Defense Appellate Division, which was housed in a commercial building in Arlington, Virginia. My wife and I, newly married in August of that year, moved from New York City to Arlington in December to start my military service.

At the time, if a soldier in the Army was convicted of a crime by a General Court Martial, he had a right to appeal to the Army's Board of Review, a tribunal composed of military officers. If the

Board of Review affirmed the conviction, then appellate counsel assigned to the case could petition the U.S. Court of Military Appeals, the highest military court, to review the case. This court was comprised of three judges appointed by the President of the United States. Like the U.S. Supreme Court, the Court of Military Appeals had discretion to grant or deny the petition. If the Court agreed to hear the case, the officer's counsel who was assigned to the case, would present oral argument before the Court of Military Appeals.

After moving into our Arlington apartment, which was a short distance to my office, I reported to the colonel in charge of the Defense Appellate Division. He explained how the cases were assigned to the twenty-four captains in the division. As the war in Vietnam was raging, he pointed out that many of our cases originated there and tended to have heavy sentences as they took place during wartime. He then proceeded to hand me the file with my first case—called *United States v. Goins*. Goins had been convicted and the Board of Review had affirmed the conviction. My predecessor counsel had already filed a petition with the Court of Military Appeals, which the court had granted. I was assigned to argue the case which was scheduled to be heard— three days hence!

I immediately sat down to read the transcript of the trial and the decision of the Board of Review. Sitting there, the enormity of my responsibility dawned on me. I am twenty-five years old, just out of law school, and my first legal experience is to deal with the life of a career soldier who was serving his sentence at Fort Leavenworth.

Reading the file, it was apparent that the case I was to argue presented a strange set of facts. As I recall them, in brief, the accused, newly arrived in Germany, was stationed at a military base not far from a wooded area where prostitutes solicited soldiers. One day, he approached a young girl who was walking on a path in the woods. Not speaking fluent German, he mouthed some German words that frightened her. As he reached out to her, she pulled out a knife and tried to stab him. He threw her on the ground. She nevertheless managed to stab him and, startled, he managed to get up before she stabbed him again. She quickly ran away.

She reported to the military authorities that Goins assaulted her. He was arraigned on a charge of attempted rape, tried, convicted, and sentenced to a bad-conduct discharge, forfeiture of all pay and allowances, and confinement at hard labor for one year. The ground for reversing that decision that predecessor counsel raised on appeal, was that the law officer who presided as a judge in the trial court erred in failing to grant a request by defense counsel to instruct the jury on the issue of self-defense. The military prosecutor joined in the request that the presiding officer instruct the jury on self-defense. Curiously, the presiding officer denied the request anyway.

For the two days I had before my court appearance, I worked on my oral argument. The defense lawyer's argument at trial and the brief filed by defendant's appellate counsel served to frame my argument. Being finally satisfied with my argument outline, I practiced before the mirror in our bathroom. I finally summoned the courage to rehearse it before my wife, hoping that if I did it enough times, my nervousness would not be so apparent to the judges.

The day of my argument, I woke up very early and practiced my argument one more time in front of the mirror. I got dressed in my military uniform, which I was going to wear for the first time, as we wore civilian clothes at the office. I walked to the office and met the colonel who was my co-counsel, but in name only. It was clear to me that he had little to do with the petition other than signing his name, and he had already advised me that he was not going to take part in the argument. Our driver got us to the court about half an hour before my appearance, which was scheduled for 11:30 a.m. As I entered the court, I got very nervous as the courthouse is similar to the Supreme Court—very majestic, even more so to a fresh out of law school twenty-five-year-old handling such a case.

We stood up as the three judges entered. After being seated, I kept looking at my notes. Finally, it was my turn to argue the case for my client. As I started to speak, the black curtain behind the chief judge parted. He swiveled his chair with his back to me, and I immediately froze, not knowing what to do. I glanced at the colonel who motioned me to continue to speak. I regained some of my composure and started my argument again. As I did so, the curtain behind one of the other judges opened. He turned away, appearing to talk to someone, and again the colonel motioned for me to continue. After a brief pause, I continued, this time without repeating myself. To my amazement, the curtain again opened behind the remaining judge, and he too turned while the others listened to my argument. When I sat down, I turned to the colonel and whispering, asked him what I did wrong. Smiling, he said "Nothing. They were just giving lunch orders to the court clerk."

In July 1967, the court (apparently having finished its lunch for the day) handed down its opinion. The judge wrote the opinion in a tongue-in-cheek manner. The opinion beginning as I recall, started something like: "The accused, chancing upon a German maiden in the woods, made advances which were met with her producing a switchblade knife with which she successfully protected her virtue." In a two-to-one decision, the court agreed with my argument that the issue of self-defense was appropriately placed in issue by the accused's defense counsel at trial and the failure of the law officer who presided at trial to instruct the court-martial jury on that issue was prejudicial error. The court reversed the decision of the Board of Review and ordered that the defendant be retried. The chief judge wrote a dissenting opinion.

I never found out whether my client was retried. I did learn a lesson that I can share with my litigating colleagues: by all means, avoid the 11:30 argument slot.

23

Off to a Good Start

by Martin S. Kaplan

Martin Kaplan is a retired partner of Wilmer Cutler Pickering Hale and Dorr, having commenced his career in 1964 at Hale and Dorr in Boston, upon graduation from Harvard Law School. He served as Chairman of the Massachusetts Board of Education (1992–96), and on the boards of the Boston Foundation, other non-profit, as well as corporate boards, and on advisory boards at Columbia, Harvard, and Yale Universities. He has held leadership positions at the American Jewish Committee and at several private foundations. This essay recounts his first major assignment at Hale and Dorr, leading to a clerkship on the U.S. Court of Appeals for the First Circuit.

I was nervous and excited to enter the old-fashioned offices of Hale and Dorr at 60 State Street in Boston on August 10, 1964, my first day of practicing law. The hiring partner showed me around the offices and introduced me to a few people. I was assigned to a small, shared office in the rabbit warren of rooms spread over two floors the firm occupied. During my first week,

I was escorted to meet Reginald Heber Smith, the then retired managing partner who gets credit for building the firm founded by Richard Hale and Dudley Dorr. Smith was a major figure nationally in the law, and is considered the father of pro bono law in America, honored ever since with his name on the major national annual legal award for pro bono practice.

For many years, I had known of Hale and Dorr, thanks to watching and admiring firm partner Joseph N. Welch take on Senator Joseph McCarthy in the televised Army-McCarthy hearings ("have you left no sense of decency, Senator"). I was thrilled to receive the offer to join the firm as an associate but sorry that Welch had died the prior October, and I never had the opportunity to meet him. Subsequently, however, I worked for, or collaborated on, many matters with both James D. St. Clair and Frederick G. Fisher, both of whom Welch had chosen to assist him in that hearing.

One morning that first week, Miss Alice Sheehan, the secretary and gatekeeper to the managing partner Paul F. Hellmuth, called and asked me to meet him in his office. That turned out to be the most important event in my entrance to law practice. Mr. Hellmuth, as I then called him, was cordial, soft-spoken and direct; I admired his style. Two or three weeks later, Miss Sheehan asked me to come meet with Mr. Hellmuth again, and I immediately went to his office. Hellmuth asked me to research a matter that set me off on a successful career at the firm.

Twentieth Century Fox had produced a film, *John Goldfarb, Please Come Home,* starring Shirley MacLaine, which made extensive use of the name and images of the nationally famous Notre Dame football team. Hellmuth was an alumnus and trustee of Notre Dame. The president of Notre Dame, Father Theodore Hesburgh, and the trustees were extremely upset that the name and reputation of Notre Dame and its football team were being used commercially, which the university would never have allowed, even if paid for the rights. Notre Dame was establishing a stellar reputation as a quality academic institution, as well as maintaining its status as a football power. The trustees believed that the public would conclude that Notre Dame had granted permission for the film to depict their football team in a silly way, when nothing could be further from the truth.

The movie depicted an American spy plane crash-landing in a Mideast nation and the subsequent imprisonment of the pilot by the king. Learning that the pilot was supposedly a Notre Dame football star, the king refuses to release him until he teaches local kids to play football. The movie then commences extensive use of the Notre Dame name and images. The movie has the U.S. State Department forcing Notre Dame to send its football team to the kingdom and the movie shows the football players wined and dined "by the King and witnessing an orgiastic entertainment provided by dancing girls from the royal harem." (Quote from later appellate decision.)

Hellmuth asked me to study case law in various jurisdictions and try to find opportunities Notre Dame might have to prevent the use of its name in the movie. I researched cases looking for one addressing whether a college could have exclusive rights to use its name and prevent its use for commercial purposes. I found a New York State case involving Cornell University, which sued Messing Bakeries, an upstate bakery that manufactured bread using the name "Cornell Bread." As Cornell had major home economics, agriculture, and hotel management schools, the university argued that using the name without approval would suggest that Cornell had endorsed that bread, and perhaps received compensation. Justice Henry Clay Greenberg, sitting in the then separate Equity Court, ruled that the bakery was unfairly trading upon the name of the university and issued a permanent injunction barring the bakery from using the name.

Relying on that case, I suggested that Notre Dame bring suit in New York, trying to tie the Notre Dame fact pattern to the Cornell case, as much as possible. However, I also warned that based on other cases, it was likely that Twentieth Century Fox would respond that they were indeed using the name Notre Dame, but only to make fun of it, and that they had a right under free speech doctrines to produce and distribute a film that included a portion that satirized college football in America.

Hellmuth had me review my draft memorandum and discuss it with two other partners whom ultimately would be considered among the best trial lawyers in the country, James D. St. Clair and Jerome P. Facher. He also arranged for me to discuss my memorandum with two prominent Harvard Law School professors, Paul Freund, perhaps the foremost constitutional scholar in the United States, and Benjamin Kaplan (not a relative), an expert in civil procedure. To say the least, this was a heady first three months in legal practice, all thanks to the assignment from Paul Hellmuth.

I also discussed my analysis with Edmund Stephan, the managing partner at the major Chicago law firm now named Mayer Brown LLP. Stephan was also the Chairman of the Notre Dame Board of Trustees. I warned that while an injunction appeared to be an appropriate result, it was very possible, even likely that courts would extend free speech rights to Twentieth Century Fox making fun of the name Notre Dame if the movie company argued that was their intent. While some attorneys thought there was not a major speech problem, I provided a separate memorandum to Hellmuth warning of my belief that the issue could ultimately prove decisive in the case.

Hellmuth took my thirty-two-page memorandum and a summary of it to a special meeting of the Notre Dame Board of Trustees, which approved suing in New York State. They retained as counsel retired New York State Judge David W. Peck, a partner at Sullivan & Cromwell. Judge Peck called me to indicate that they were going to sue using my analysis, but he was delaying filing the suit from November until December 1. I asked why, and he answered "because the judge sitting in equity jurisdiction in New York State Supreme Court in Manhattan as of December 1 is going be . . . Henry Clay Greenberg." I gulped and smiled.

Twentieth Century Fox and its counsel Rogers & Wells, fell into a trap their client had set for themselves, as it became clear to Justice Greenberg that the use of the name Notre Dame was only because its fame would help sell tickets and encourage interest in the movie. Judge Greenberg entered an injunction against the movie being shown, ruining its hope for year-end Christmas season ticket sales. Citing Warren and Brandeis "The Right to Privacy," Greenberg held "that the legal concept of property comprehends an interest in one's name, symbols, and all that they connote," and quoting from his own Cornell decision repeated that "an educational institution which has won large public prestige by hard effort and at high cost ought not, against its will, have that prestige diluted by a commercial use of its name . . . ."

Justice Greenberg also wrote that "the property right so enumerated, however, is not an absolute one" and recognized the public's "right to know" and the breadth of freedom of speech and of the press, but held "by their own urgings, and the Court agrees upon a reading of the book and picture script, neither the book nor the motion picture itself is a satire, burlesque or any other form of literary portrayal or criticism of Notre Dame or its team, nor does it represent an educational, cultural, moral, or sociological crusade in the public welfare."

Greenberg concluded that "the glaringly evident purpose and effect of defendants' tacking on of the name and symbols of Notre Dame were to capitalize on the commercial value such name and symbols had acquired in the minds of the consuming public. This is a clear case of commercial piracy, and in no way is this decision intended to, nor does it restrict the legitimate conduct of the press or the expression of free speech."

Immediately after that decision, Twentieth Century Fox dropped Rogers & Wells as counsel and hired retired Judge Samuel Rosenman, former counsel to President Franklin D. Roosevelt and senior partner at Rosenman & Colin. He took the appeal to the Appellate Division of the Supreme Court of New York, and the case was then further appealed to the highest court in New York State, the Court of Appeals. He argued that the appellate courts should disregard the evidence suggesting that the use of the name was solely or primarily for commercial purposes. Rosenman contended that the case was one of free speech and satire, and won the support of most of the judges in the two appellate courts.

Justice Bernard Botein writing for a unanimous appellate division, stated that the movie was a farce and "there is no possibility whatever" that anyone could conceivably believe that the book and movie were associated in any official capacity with Notre Dame. He further stated that if the injunction remained in force, its effect would be to "outlaw large areas heretofore deemed permissible subject matter for literature and the arts." None of that opinion surprised me except Botein's total disregard of the evidence offered by both parties in the equity hearing before Justice Greenberg

Notre Dame appealed to the Court of Appeals, which affirmed the decision by a vote of 4–2 without issuing any written opinion. That inspired a strong dissent by Associate Judge Adrian P. Burke who argued for himself and one other dissenter that "To us it is obvious that, because defendants have admittedly taken the name and symbols of Notre Dame and its football team repeatedly throughout their productions, readers and viewers are likely to think Notre Dame was connected with the enterprise and that Notre Dame and would be irreparably harmed thereby. Certainly, with the script calling for actual film clips of the real Notre Dame team in action, the remarks in *Sports Illustrated*, and the admission of the producer . . . , the question whether rational readers or viewers could draw such an inference should be at least a triable issue."

Twentieth Century Fox had tried to dissuade Notre Dame from bringing the suit by showing that the team was not depicted in a negative way and invited Hesburgh, Hellmuth and other trustees to come to New York to see the movie prior to its release. Hellmuth was kind enough to invite me, an associate of all of three months, to come to New York with him and meet the president and several trustees of Notre Dame. I reluctantly explained that I couldn't come because my wife and I were expecting our first child to be born within the next couple days. And, indeed, our first child was born that next evening.

I happened to see Father Hesburgh at the Harvard Faculty Club around the year 2000 and reminded him of the movie and the litigation. He informed me that Twentieth Century Fox was so angry at losing the Christmas business because of the injunction that they insisted on obtaining payment of their legal fees since they succeeded in overturning the injunction. He told me it cost Notre Dame a quarter of a million dollars. That was a giant sum in the mid-1960s—the equivalent today of over two million dollars.

The Notre Dame case was certainly a fortuitous way to start my career at Hale and Dorr. It became even more important than I thought when it led directly to my becoming a clerk to Chief Judge Bailey Aldrich on the U.S. Court of Appeals for the First Circuit in Boston.

At that time, the First Circuit Court (with Federal jurisdiction in Massachusetts, Rhode Island, New Hampshire, Maine, and the Virgin Islands) had three judges, but Judge Aldrich was the only sitting judge as the other two positions had become vacant. Judge Aldrich decided he needed a second clerk, and in November wrote the managing partners of five Boston law firms seeking recommendations for a clerk to join his office on January

1. Hellmuth nominated me and I was chosen by Judge Aldrich following an interview. Thus, thanks to working for Hellmuth and Notre Dame, I became a clerk to a chief judge of one of the U.S. Courts of Appeals, one of the more prestigious clerkships available to graduating law students.

Paul Hellmuth remained a mentor to me during my time as an associate and young partner, and brought me into several important client relationships and matters. When he took early retirement, I succeeded him in maintaining those clients and followed his tradition of being a strategic advisor to clients and families over many years. I also emulated him in his commitment to the community and society by being active on boards of nonprofit organizations.

I learned a great deal from Judge Aldrich. I took notes during oral argument of cases on which I was his clerk, and observed him and counsel closely. He insisted on thorough research of law, solid analysis of the facts, detailed study of the briefs, all to be done on a timely, often expedited, basis. He held his clerks to high standards and was clear in his directions and expectations. He was firm but gentle, just as he was a soft-spoken but forceful presence on that court, and the model of a great judge.

I occasionally considered what it would be like to have a judicial career but that's not the course my career took. Instead, I chose a life of serving as an attorney and strategic advisor to corporate clients, and as a trustee and counselor to individuals, families, and foundations, as well as being active in society on corporate and non-profit boards and active in politics and public service. I was inspired in those directions by the example of Hellmuth and several other partners at Hale and Dorr.

24

Good Intentions

by Roger M. Witten

It began with a call from a lawyer at a well-regarded firm asking whether I could assist her in advising her firm's client about a question that related to a U.S. federal law called The Foreign Corrupt Practices Act, which, to simplify, makes it a crime for certain people and companies to bribe a foreign government official. I was more than happy to lend a hand.

In connection with that engagement, I met a senior executive of what I will call "Foreign Bank." A short while later, Foreign Bank called seeking to retain me to give it advice relating to the same law, the FCPA .

In the call, Foreign Bank was vague about the nature of the issue they wanted to retain me to address. The bank urged me to come to its headquarters many time zones away to meet the Bank's senior team.

He also said he suspected that their phones were being tapped so we had to use code names. I gave everyone the name of a major league baseball team. So, we had the Cardinal, the Blue Jay, the Oriole, etc.

In due course, I made the long trek to meet them. They

planned a heavy agenda of meetings and entertainment with various apparently important persons, but they usually didn't tell me who I was seeing or why until I just about arrived at the meeting site. In several meetings, I received interesting briefings on the country's economy, geography, ethnic groups, etc.

From time to time thereafter, the Foreign Bank senior executive called me, often in the middle of the night EST—a time when I found it difficult to remember who was the Cardinal and who was the Oriole, etc. Typically, in these calls, they asked for information about developments or officials in Washington.

This went on for a year or two.

Finally, in one of these calls, they told me that they had reached the strategic conclusion that U.S. investment in their country would continue to be very limited unless the country addressed the corruption issue. Without U.S. and other Western investment, the country's economy and standard of living would remain low. The bank clearly had the acumen to see that its long-term commercial interests aligned with sound public policy.

Foreign Bank asked me to devise a strategy to address corruption in that country. This job, which in other countries would be performed by the equivalent of the Minister of Justice or legislative leaders, had to be done outside of government circles because it was politically explosive and, moreover, because lawyers in the country lacked the requisite expertise.

So, three of us from the law firm undertook to draft legislation. We came up with a structure that was based in part on features of South Africa's post-apartheid Truth and Reconciliation Commission, and in part on claims settlement structures used to distribute compensation to Holocaust survivors. The central idea was to induce corrupt officials to "come clean" in return for which they would receive immunity.

We returned to the country and, as before, we were hustled to meetings whose participants and subject matters were not disclosed to us until we were in the car on the way. One meeting seemed to be with the equivalent of the country's attorney general. This meeting was held in secret in a hotel room because it was apparently risky for him to be seen with us in his office.

Shakespeare in *Macbeth* referred to "sound and fury signifying nothing." And that was what it was here. After all our exertions, nothing was done. Foreign Bank did not, to my knowledge, thereafter pursue an anticorruption initiative, deeming it too risky to proceed. It was just too heavy a lift.

ABOUT THE EDITOR

Roger Witten graduated from Dartmouth College and Harvard Law School. On the suggestion of a law school professor, Archibald Cox, he secured a clerkship with Judge Harrison Winter, who sat on the U.S. Court of Appeals for the Fourth Circuit in Baltimore.

The clerkship was cut short when Professor Cox became the Watergate Special Prosecutor. Judge Winter graciously recommended that Witten join Cox's embryonic staff, which Witten soon thereafter did.

At the Watergate Special Prosecution Force, Witten worked on the campaign finance team, which prosecuted about twenty companies and individuals including Herbert Kalmbach who was President Nixon's personal lawyer and a fundraiser as well as Maurice Stans who had been Secretary of Commerce and headed President Nixon's reelection finance committee.

In 1975, Witten joined Wilmer Cutler & Pickering. He practiced in both Washington, D.C. and New York City. Witten later headed the firm's litigation practice, acted as the senior partner in the New York office, and served on the firm's Management Committee.

Witten's areas of expertise were: 1) large-scale litigation typically with international dimensions; 2) internal corporate investigations which again typically had international dimensions; 3) the Foreign Corrupt Practices Act; 4) white-collar criminal matters, often relating to the FCPA; and 5) on a pro bono basis, campaign finance reform for clients that included Senators McCain, Feingold, and van Hollen, Common Cause, Democracy 21, and the Campaign Legal Center. Witten authored or co-authored numerous professional articles on these topics and was the lead author of a treatise "Complying with the Foreign Corrupt Practices Act," now in its tenth edition. Witten has received a number of professional accolades.

Witten has been married to Jill Witten for over fifty years. They have two daughters and four grandchildren.

ACKNOWLEDGMENTS

I couldn't have completed this book without the help and encouragement of many people, including the essayists who agreed to participate and worked hard, even when it was unclear, to say the least, that this adventure would end happily; my wife, Jill, who encouraged me to invest my time and our money in this project; the many friends whose wise counsel and encouragement was very valuable, including Arthur Ainsburg , John Briggs, and Mark Kessel among others; and, of course, the Easton Studio Press team including David Wilk and Jeremy Townsend.